SPEAK KINDLY

TO YOUR

SHADOW

THE ART OF REFRAMING
THE DIVINE

Sandra Anne Davis

SPEAK KINDLY TO YOUR SHADOW: THE ART OF REFRAMING THE DIVINE
Copyright © 2025 by Sandra Anne Davis

All rights reserved. No part of this book may be reproduced or transmitted in any form or by any means without written permission from the author.

For more information visit:
www.writingfortheloveofit.com

Copyediting by Emma Května

ISBN: 978-1-7782729-2-9

First Edition: October 2025

DEDICATION

This book is dedicated to all my clients, my family and friends. Your bravery and courage are genuine examples of this human experience. With true humility, you offer a reflection of the magnificence that you are…and that we are as a humanity. Any societal perception of frailties is debunked by your very nature!

In memory of Richard Gordon Davis who died on Saturday, May 18th 2024 at Hospice Fredericton and in gratitude of the hospice initiative, half of the proceeds from this book will be donated to any hospice in Canada wishing to partner with Sandra.

TABLE OF CONTENTS

DEDICATION 3

INTRODUCTION 7

CHAPTER ONE: BUILDING A NEW FOUNDATION .. 16

    GOD: Governing Oneself Divinely 16

    What does Responsibility mean? 22

    The Authentic Witness 27

    What's it all for? 35

    Putting It All Together 39

CHAPTER TWO: THE CLIMB 44

    The Cocoon of Defiance 50

    My 'Not Enoughness' 60

    Awakened By Angels 64

    The Sweat Lodge Experience 72

CHAPTER THREE: THE VISION QUEST 79

    The Boy in the White Dress 82

    The Little Tree 87

    The Cave Fire 93

    Medicine Man Sharing Circle 95

CHAPTER FOUR: THE ART OF REFRAMING THE DIVINE 105

The Gift of Mirrors 105
Making The Not Personal, Personal.............112
The Power of Words: Reframing Concepts with Acronyms 120
Having Faith..127
How Not To Run Away.................................131

CHAPTER FIVE: DEATH, THE UNPLANNED CHAPTER 143

A Love Story Completed...............................143
Death and Life Go Together.........................151
Choice Lives On 154

CHAPTER SIX: AN INVITATION TO REFRAME 158

You, Too, Can Reframe 158
Consulting With Yourself 160
The Shadow Speaks 166

AFTERWORD **176**

RESOURCES **181**

ENDNOTES..**182**

INTRODUCTION

When writing a book, you might ask yourself—Why? Why this book? And why now? What is the intention? What has ignited your passion and is demanding an alternative rhythm in your heart? These are the words of my sage, my editor Emma Května…wise words indeed.

There are two reasons why I have chosen to write this book. First, it is the culmination of my philosophy on how to live life and what I have discovered through a process I call 'reframing'. Through a willingness to surrender and release any previous perception I held of the Shadow—a dark and unknown place within me that I knew little about—I was able to discover a new understanding of myself, and how I interacted with the world; it was motivation to become more specific, more present, and most significantly, more authentic!

Speaking of being authentic, this idea of 'speaking kindly to my shadow' actually came from my beautiful husband Rick. One day during morning meditation, I felt compelled to share my writings and discuss my thoughts with him. Rick was always happy to be my muse. After our discussion, Rick went back to his chair in the den and I went back to meditating. Soon after that, Rick returned. He put his hand on my right shoulder and whispered, "Speak kindly to your shadow" then walked back to his chair. I got it! Thanking him I replied, "This is the perfect title for my book." It was in Rick's moment of inspiration that he so aptly and succinctly formulated the expression I desired to share of my philosophy. What wisdom!

The second reason for writing this manuscript is that the result of this philosophy of reframing, and the successful application of it, has led to many of my clients, friends, and family members requesting that I write a book describing how reframing works and how it benefits our daily lives. Providing a written explanation of this tool and how it works to improve lives on a daily basis makes perfect sense for further understanding.

It has been an honour and a privilege to apply reframing directly in my life and share it with clients through my knowledge and experience. In my capacity as a Spiritual Counsellor[i] I have been able to provide concrete examples of reframing situations as they arise in the lives of those I am counselling. Their personal experience with reframing is ongoing. And so, here seems as good a place as any to invite you to join us!

I feel the best place to begin with is the collective belief many people hold in the illusion of being separate from anything or anyone. This illusion was the culprit that kept me distanced from myself and others. A saboteur that robbed me of peace, "the peace of God that surpasses all understanding" (The Bible, Philippians 4:7).

Through the recognition and guidance of my Shadow, I was able to develop the tool of reframing. Equipped with a new understanding of the world and my place in it, I began to cease my habit of sabotaging my own well-being and allowed Spirit to become my new GPS. It graciously led me to the following quote:

"I no longer try to change outer things. They are simply a reflection. I change my inner perception and the outer reveals the beauty so long obscured by my own attitude. I concentrate on my inner vision and find my outer view transformed. I find myself attuned to the grandeur of life and in unison with the perfect order of the universe." (*The Book of Runes*, Page 132, Ralph H, Blum, St. Martin's Press New York)

SPEAK KINDLY TO YOUR SHADOW

This quote sparked an innate recognition within me. An understanding that it is timely to engage in the power of intention for me…the whole of me. The compassion I exhibit and the grace with which I determine the worth and magnificence of others, must now be reframed and applied to myself.

A personal pursuit of intimacy with myself, illuminated challenges with those whom I was relating to. Clarity and insightfulness emerged with every interaction. My dealings with others were no longer confrontational. It was respectful and honourable. The shift was a simple one but the outcome was profound! Everything was more real, more genuine.

The courage to pursue a better way to effectively navigate my life created the change I was seeking. By listening to the yearning of my soul, the struggle to relate in life with love and friendship in all my exchanges—vanished. This was the offering of a new way, a blueprint, a map for the journey.

I felt a stirring, a genuine desire to reach out to the hand being offered—my hand! The hand of my Shadow, the aspect of me that is the authentic witness. She is not compromised by anything. No emotions, no drama, and no desires. Most significantly, no attachment to resolution or outcome. Hallelujah! For there were times when this pilgrim did not choose the path of least resistance. Hell, if there was a sign with no writing on it, only remnants of faded letters, I would surely choose it! To say there were times I was well-battered and thoroughly bruised would not be an understatement. But my newfound intimacy with my soul allowed me to trust in a simpler, less painful way that met the desire for peace within me.

When I look into the eyes of my Shadow, the depth of the green "I" witness reminds me to reflect on the colour green and what it means to me. Heart; the fourth chakra. The pump needed for the physical body, the feeling body, and the spiritual body. Without the steady beat and rhythm of my heart, each of these areas becomes erratic, compromising the whole and obscuring the very existence of this authentic witness.

This observation highlighted my need for alignment. There are many conditions of the heart that compromise my needs and complicate my genuine desire for balance. The most prevalent is a lack of self-worth, created by the belief that I am not enough! A belief of being somehow deficient and wanting. This belief compromises the choices I make for myself and my life's journey, robbing me of a true present! It also serves to reinforce the belief itself.

So how do I root out and eradicate this belief and many others that give life and feed energy to my well-developed ego? Ah, ego – my other companion! But we'll get to that later…

With this manuscript, it is my intention to share with you how I made magic in my life simply by reframing what I understood of the nature of reality! And the nature of love. Paraphrasing my Cherokee Feast of Days Daily Meditation book:

"Nothing has power against strong words. 'I will seek that which was lost, and bring again that which was driven away, and will bind up that which was broken, and will strengthen that which was sick.' And then we can ride the waves of our emotions like a canoe and not get upset among the waves." (Joyce Sequichie Hifler, pg 25)

And so it is with this quote that we begin the journey of reframing and meeting the Shadow. It is now time to unzip the cloak of deception and reveal the authentic, the real self; that which resides within us. Unnoticed. An unsung heroine. Yet connected wholly and completely as one with source, with God.

SPEAK KINDLY TO YOUR SHADOW

Recently I came across these words written by Leah Schell:

"Words composed and written honestly with charity and daring are magic, alchemy, and fragments of starlight. They are gold dust and whisperings of the soul caught in ink and paper to enchant and inspire those that gaze upon them." I was besotted!

This description of words explained to me how I came to fall in love with the written word and why I have been in pursuit of their meaning my entire life. It coloured my perception and commanded my heart to beat in rhythm with a collective unconscious that was now being revealed to me. Leah Schell is the artist that shared her brushes with me, with all of us.

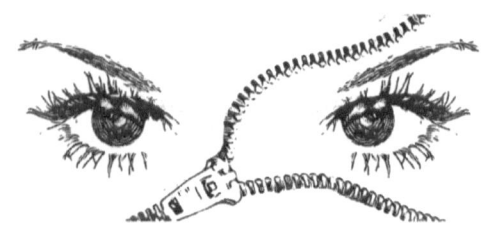

CHAPTER ONE: BUILDING A NEW FOUNDATION

GOD: GOVERNING ONESELF DIVINELY

The overall goal of reframing **is *self-love*…**plain and simple!

In order for me to explain the concept of reframing, I must first start with my realization that without self-love, love cannot exist! How can anyone love another without first knowing through experience, what love is? I do believe that this has been God's intention from the beginning.

Does this actually mean what I think it means? Have I spent my life believing that I was exercising love in my dealings with others, but because I had no experience of loving myself, what I understood of love was actually an illusion? The answer is an affirmative *"Yes!"*

I found this epiphany difficult to embrace. It implies so many truths that set my teeth on edge. Certainly, within the framework of religion and cultural affiliations—all these beliefs are based on me loving God, something I believed I was doing for the entirety of my life…the one surety throughout my earthly sojourn, the very bedrock of my foundation! And yet, with this new epiphany, all of my beliefs around loving God came into question. What was I to do with this newfound understanding? How could I come to terms with it?

Fortunately, through my exposure to the ways of the Medicine Wheel and guidance from the angels, the reshaping of my world has been successful, albeit gradual.

The Medicine Wheel is sometimes called the Sacred Hoop[ii]. This symbol of all of life's cycles provided the First Indigenous People an evolutionary blueprint for centuries. Each cycle of life is honoured in a sacred way, allowing us to see the value of each step on our pathway, and a new understanding of our growth patterns. Each person's unique experience is a way for other members to see varied themes in the same lesson; in other words, we all serve to *mirror*.

The Medicine Wheel is the circle of lessons that each person must pass through to complete their journey on the Good Red Road of physical life. *"The Medicine Wheel is the blueprint for all situations…including the return to new physical lives via the Blue Road of Spirit"* (Sacred Path Cards, Jamie Sams. page 83, 84, 85). I will

SPEAK KINDLY TO YOUR SHADOW

include some of the reference material that I relied upon in the endnotes of this book for those of you who would like to read and develop your own understanding of The Medicine Wheel.

I have determined that a significant aspect of the Medicine Wheel is the extraordinary ability to spiral deep within that it provides us with, where it magnetizes what no longer serves our journey, gathering all that has been buried, all that has become a liability! Because nature abhors a vacuum[iii] the Shadow then gifts us with reflection, revealing those unstudied places within, by way of external *mirrors* (other people, other situations).

Thus, it is largely, though not entirely, through Medicine Wheel teachings that I was able to come to a new understanding of God and soothe my newfound concerns around my lack of self-love in light of loving God. Though my rudimentary understanding of God has changed over the years, my desire to know and love God has remained strong enough to endure. One perception of God that has developed and continues to sustain me is the following acronym: **G**overning **O**neself **D**ivinely. There is no religious or cultural connotation in this definition. It is about self-governance and self-responsibility—it's all about the self, the 'I'. But, be assured, the 'I' is not, nor can it ever be separate from God! Rather, it's that God and I are one. This is what I have come to recognize as true **sovereignty**.

With an understanding of this *reframe*, I could fully embrace the importance of loving myself! Self-love is loving God because God is all-present, and is everything and everyone in this world, as am I. The moment I experience the emotion of disdain, dislike, judgement or hatred towards any aspect of life such as another person or a situation, I can know with certainty that I'm responding from a place of separation. *Reacting* might be a better descriptor. Regardless, what I am doing is directing these emotions at myself (and God). There is no separation; they are one in the same!

I like the analogy of 'I' being a wave in the ocean of God. And as a wave in this ocean, I'm not the sum total of the whole ocean. As much as I recognize myself as a wave in the ocean of God, I am also aware that it isn't possible for me to understand the ocean as a whole, being only the wave that I am.

What I can do, however, is choose! Choose to experience everything in my life with this new understanding. If governing oneself divinely is my purpose, then I can choose to live my life *on purpose*! Happily, and with gratitude **I can accept the responsibility for conducting myself and my life**. This was to be yet another catalyst, one that would change my life completely! By embracing this analogy during self-excavation, the tool of *reframing* became the flashlight at my disposal.

SANDRA ANNE DAVIS

WHAT DOES RESPONSIBILITY MEAN?

In the words of my Medicine teacher "Woody" responsibility means the *ability to respond in any situation.* **Read that again slowly, because it's important:** Responsibility simply means the ***ability* to *respond* in any situation.** Yet, the idea of 'responsibility' often makes those of us of the human persuasion *shrink!* We as a society have developed a mistaken belief that responsibility is heavy, burdensome and even oppressive. Like others, I too have shared this collective perception thereby adding to my subjective experience of suffering. Here I find it interesting that the word "suffering" in its original sense, merely means "undergoing" as interpreted by Ralph H. Blum in *The Book of Runes*. Yet another example of the way in which society manifests from a state of unconsciousness!

SPEAK KINDLY TO YOUR SHADOW

However, reframing provided the light I needed in order to see that the <u>weight of the word</u> "responsibility" was *perceptual* and of my own making! This word, like all words, is benign, until it is determined otherwise by me (the user). Simply by reframing my previous perception of responsibility, I was able to accept that I possessed the ***ability to respond in any situation***. I felt a burden lift. I was now able to see that my ill-gotten perception of responsibility was actually distancing me from 'Self'. Going forward I chose daily to embrace this ability in every situation!

The ability to respond is activated through governing oneself and choosing to be an expression of love. God is love and love is God expressed in the world! There's no separation from God and love. No more than there is a separation from myself, God and others. I am a wave, an aspect of God (the ocean), and like that wave, my expression in the world changes based on how I'm perceiving things. And like all waves, I too have varying forms of expression: calm, turbulent, flowing, thrashing, quiet. However, Shadow (which we will explore more in the next section) is not a form of expression. Shadow just *is*. Like God. Like love.

But what about ego? One may think that ego gets in the way of being responsible in life, because when we have a big ego, we feel separate from others and thus, may feel entitled to absolve ourselves of any responsibility! But even ego is just terminology to describe an aspect of the self that serves us in this human incarnation. Yes, that's right—ego serves us! Ego provides knowledge about identity of self and what it means to be human, for one cannot know who one is without reflection (Carl Jung, *The Undiscovered Self,* 1957). And the power of family and society offers the perfect gift of *mirrors* since we all have an ego. Once we can *see* our ego, we can choose to decenter it and take back the ability to *respond authentically* in any given situation.

When seeking spiritual understanding, one often feels it is their duty to "kill off the ego" and control its impulses. A common reaction is to feel disdain, disgust and disrespect <u>even for the word</u> "ego". But who are we to judge any aspect of ourselves? The moment we judge something, we're judging the whole, which puts the expression of 'God as love' out of balance, because love and judgement cannot reside within the same energy; they have differing vibrations.

I have come to recognize and understand that illusion has become reality for society! And subsequently I've experienced an immense sense of loss, the loss of true substance. There is nothing solid to brace myself on in a power stance, no surety to base my faith upon! It appears most people don't want the responsibility of governing one's self, divinely or otherwise. It's easier to believe in the victim mindset than to believe that there are no victims, only volunteers. Because we all signed up for this life. When we saw that big clip board saying Life on Earth, we knew what a gift we were in for. The opportunity to experience life, to be alive and take that first breath on this planet. With an open heart we said "Sign me up!"

By choosing sovereignty (self-governance), we are making a choice to govern ourselves divinely. We're expressing the truth of God through the energy of love. It is not my intention to imply this is the *only* right choice, since choice is all there is, but we can, however, come to recognize governing ourselves divinely as an option.

So, what does this have to do with the Shadow and reframing? Well clearly, if I'm going to learn to love myself, and the goal of reframing is love in all its forms, reframing is the perfect tool for recognizing and understanding responsibility! Shadow reflects everything! This is its only purpose: making what is unknown…known. Exposing the where and how of love's existence and the truth of its *absence*. Shadow asks nothing of us. It only reveals what has been cloaked; our perceived mistakes, faults, challenges, beliefs, our blessings, even our magnificence and our perceptions of one another.

THE AUTHENTIC WITNESS

Let's start reframing by befriending our Shadow. What exactly is the Shadow and its role in our life?

She is the authentic witness to our life. She is always there…the eternal feminine balance, the invisible authentic counterpart necessary for *truth, growth* and *integrity.*

Imagine, if you will, that you're on a stage and everything behind you is dark so that *you* become all there is. The darkness behind you is the Shadow, holding that space for you to perform in. Through her gift of being a witness, the Shadow sees all aspects of you—the injured, the orphaned child within, the saboteur, the wounded healer, our fears, the imposter, the warrior, hopes and dreams; all the parts we choose to play and experience. She holds a space for us to visit those places within us, to look at those aspects of our perception that we don't face every day.

So, if you're holding a perception that you're not aware of, then you've unconsciously cloaked that perception. But your Shadow sees it. She sees everything! Faithfully, she remains ready for you when you want to remove the veil of separation and expose your authenticity. However unnatural this may feel, this reflection is for your highest good and the highest good of all—it's a gift!

There is an angel doll story from my book *Angels Do The Darndest Things* that offers a beautiful metaphor about beliefs that are unconscious, yet observed by the Shadow.

SPEAK KINDLY TO YOUR SHADOW

Through the personal experience of my friend Linda Penn, and the angel doll that she commissioned from our friend Elsie Poloquin, we are provided with a glimpse of the perceptions that have quite literally been cloaked! I will tell you the story now, which is paraphrased from my other book *Angels Do The Darndest Things* in the chapter called "White Wolf Woman: Angel of Forgiveness".

Elsie created an angel doll for Linda called White Wolf Woman. This angel doll was created in the image of an Indigenous medicine woman with a walking stick, to assist Linda in walking her talk. White Wolf Woman wore a beautiful buckskin outfit trimmed with intricate beadwork. She had long black hair that was braided and elegant with white feathered wings. Her beauty was undeniable, yet Linda found herself unsettled and even angry at seeing the doll wearing a rabbit fur cloak, because Linda held a belief that rabbits symbolize fear. Linda felt that White Wolf

Woman represented her, or at least some aspect of her, and therefore, she was in denial that the beautiful, wise, knowing woman inside of herself was cloaked in fear.

Other than the rabbit fur cloak, Linda loved the doll and found her introduction to the White Wolf aspect of herself very comforting. Through her knowledge of wolf medicine being that of a teacher, and white representing sacredness, this angel doll creation seemed the perfect reflection of Linda's journey. And so, the solution for Linda was simple; she would ask Elsie to remove the rabbit fur cloak.

Well, much to her surprise and dismay, Elsie's response was a firm, "All is appropriate. This is what I was guided to place upon her and there is a reason for it!" In that moment, it became crystal clear to Linda that she had to face the fact that her wisdom was cloaked in fear.

White Wolf Woman sat on the mantle of Linda's fireplace for over a year, during which time Linda made every effort to work on her fears. Then one day Linda returned home to find that her Siamese cat named 'Freedom' had torn off the rabbit fur cloak and destroyed it! As Linda investigated the destruction further, she discovered that the only thing damaged on the angel doll was in fact the cloak and nothing else...*Wow!* In that moment and with absolute certainty, Linda realized that she had successfully worked through her fears and had forgiven her choices. She was now ready to walk her talk.

What an inspiring and powerful lesson gifted to Linda by our dear friend and very wise teacher Elsie Poloquin. *May she rest in peace; deceased in 2018.*

Through Linda's story, I hope you can see that reframing is about recognizing the gift in the current situation, and being brave and courageous enough to allow ourselves the freedom to see what we are most afraid to look at—like Linda's Siamese cat Freedom so obligingly provided!

Now, I do not have a cat named Freedom, so for me, the beauty and strength needed for uncloaking my own repressed perceptions came through the experience of confrontation; having someone literally in my face, absolutely raging and screaming at me!

This kind of moment is when I take a deep breath, pause, and be still. I just allow that person to run off steam, because eventually they'll wear themselves out. It can be challenging because we all have boundaries and feel entitled to be treated a certain way. But witnessing, like peace, is not a practice; it's an act of patience. This patience developed within me the more I exercised it, and it uncloaked my unconscious perceptions around judgement and my lack of compassion towards others. I'm now able to keep myself separate from judging others. I separate from the idea of threat and disengage lovingly and without judgement (most of the time; I'm human after all!), choosing instead to remember the words of the Tibetan Buddhist teacher Kongtrul Rinpoche: "Even though we may make a lot of mistakes and we mess up in all kinds of ways...fundamentally, our minds and hearts are not guilty. They are innocent." (pp. 96-97, *Practicing Peace In Times Of War,* Pema Chödrön, 2006).

This I believe to be true! Through a desire to respond with love and a commitment to exercising compassion and grace, arguments and tumultuous experiences decreased in my life. Those experiences were a mirror provided by Shadow that allowed me to see that I no longer desired those types of relationships and interactions, and that I was the *only* one who could change them! I came to understand as a direct result of patience that all exchanges were for my highest good and the highest good of others, or they simply would not be a reflection in my life. Through my willingness to reframe the actions of others, judgment was removed from the equation and true liberation was my reward.

But how, you might ask, do I know if I'm being truly loving in a situation, especially when I've determined a need to implement a boundary and am acting accordingly? If you can interact with someone without judgement, that's it! That's the answer, pure and simple. In the words of The Beatles hit 1967 single: *"All you need is love, love is all you need."* When everything that is not love is absent, all that remains is love. Just as compassion cannot exist within judgement, love cannot exist *without* compassion.

To really grasp this, it's important to understand that compassion and empathy are *not* the same thing. You don't have to be empathetic to someone's situation in order to bear witness or refrain from judging. Nor do you have to buy into any situation the person may be expressing about. All you have to do is witness without judgement and recognize that they are serving you and your highest good by mirroring those deep places of <u>self-loathing</u> back to you. With this newfound knowledge, you will be better able to accept their gift of showing you *the places you have not yet found the courage to visit or reveal within yourself!*

Their willingness to mirror your own insecurities, your fears and even your untapped rage, is a genuine act of bravery! By choosing to reflect aspects of yourself that you are unwilling to look at and take ownership of, their willingness to play this role, to offer this mirror, makes it easier for us to release judgement and sit in the place of compassion. Not compassion for the person you're interacting with; just compassion, *end of story.*

WHAT'S IT ALL FOR?

So, if Shadow is the authentic witness to life, and if we are here to bear witness to each other, and all of it comes down to making the choice <u>to take responsibility for governing oneself divinely</u>, what is it all in effort for? Again, in the words of John Lennon, *"All you need is love!"*

Through the Shadow's gift of authenticity, we are able to fine-tune what it means to be present, which allows us to tap into love—<u>the source of God</u>. **Love is God expressed in the world**. But to reach that authentic experience with love, you must make a choice to do so.

When I'm expressing my authentic self, I'm expressing God through my words, deeds and thoughts. If I become an expression of God in the world, then I'm as real and as authentic as I can be since God is the source of everything.

Learning to love is all we're here for. It's a fulfilling pursuit because it's how we really know that we exist. In the forefront of your mind, always keep the notion that there is perhaps no greater expression of the love that you are than when you act in the best interest of and for the highest good of all! When you choose to live and work this way, you are the magician; a true alchemist, shaping and redefining the world you live in. Never doubt the contribution you are making to the whole!

We come to understand that we aren't here randomly and we aren't here by mistake; we fit in. Through love, we can come to understand that we *do* exist and that we're amazing, magnificent and absolutely perfect in our imperfections. The journey is perfect. As the playwright, the author of the book, we are scripting the journey. When you recognize how powerful and magnificent that is, and you honour every bit of it, then you simply make choices that reflect this understanding.

But Sandra, you might ask, that all sounds well and good, but why does it *matter* that I know I exist? I mean in the grander scheme of life, why is it important?

I can only answer with a question from author and lawyer-turned-spiritual-teacher Arnold Patent: *"How is God to know God without us?"* In other words, if we didn't exist, how would God, or source, ever be able to know itself? In this way, we as a whole are like the authentic witness for God. Collectively, we are holding that space so that God can experience God. Because how do you recognize the magnificence of wholeness if you don't have the experience of lacking it in the first place? How do you recognize perfection without imperfection? How does <u>wind know that it is wind</u> until it moves a branch's leaves? This is how our Shadow teaches us. She holds space for the reflection of me looking in the mirror and seeing that I exist, and how I go about existing.

The only way to get to that place where you can pause long enough to look in the mirror is to be in the vibration of love. That's why the experience of love cannot be confined by conditions. <u>If you confine it, you lose it</u>. You can't love anything until you love yourself. And you can't truly love anything if there are conditions. As soon as you say "I love you, but I wish you wouldn't do that" then the love is no longer present. You may say you love your dog—until they pee on the carpet! There's a difference between loving a person or object in relation to them with conditions, and simply being in the vibration of love all the time, regardless.

PUTTING IT ALL TOGETHER

Let's review! The purpose of us incarnating as humans is so that God can know God.

God can be understood as love expressed, and governing ourselves divinely through responsibility and choice.

But God is not a separate entity. There is no separation between God and I, God and you, God and everything, though our human conduct and thoughts would have us believe otherwise. We transcend this human conduct when we remember that we have an amazing tool called *reframing*, which allows us to see the gift in any given moment or situation.

Reframing helps us see that we are simply here to bear witness to one another, without judgement, within compassion, as the reflection of love that we are. We can do this by becoming present through prayer and meditation (stillness or movement) so that we can listen, feel and align with our own authentic witness—our Shadow.

When we speak kindly to our Shadow—*she who sees all that life is*—we receive wise insight from deep inside and all around us. It begins with a new and very personal conversation with our Shadow, first and foremost. If we can't love our Shadow, our ego, or our self, then we are unable to authentically bear witness for others, and love them and love life.

SPEAK KINDLY TO YOUR SHADOW

For instance, by listening to my Shadow, she wisely taught me that hope is a valuable commodity without limitations! This insight forced me to question the meaning of hope because hope is something we all have, whether we believe in it or not. Psychologist Denise Larsen has studied hope for 18 years and defines it as *"the ability to envision a future that we wish to participate in."* How powerful is that? In order to witness others, love without judgment, and be in a state of compassion, one must have hope—hope that we all collectively get to a place where love as a state of being is the *norm*, and we are no longer limited by our minds.

However, there was a time in my life where I was unaware of the necessity of hope and its capacity to motivate my pursuit of a life without limitations! This would have been early on, before my deep-seated desire for unification became conscious. And so, I've decided to share some very personal experiences with you, my readers, to provide you with insight and clarity. By sharing aspects of my own journey of reframing—fragments, actually—it is my desire that you will gain a better understanding relative to the journey that is uniquely yours.

SPEAK KINDLY TO YOUR SHADOW

*"Confession may be good for the soul, but it seldom makes the one that heard it feel good. The need to clear the air or get something out in the open can cause a bigger rift than the reason for confessing in the first place. Words cannot be retrieved once they are spoken. They are gone and calling them back is impossible. Some weigh on people's hearts like **hi lv s gi nv ya**, many stones or heavy rock. Some are flung, like **di ga ti s di,** a spear, to wound. And most should never have been spoken. Life and death are in the use of words. If we feel the need to confess something, we should do it where the listener knows how to handle what we say. It is an unthinking person that needs to be relieved of a burden to the point of putting it on someone who may find it hard to bear."*

Cherokee Feast of Days, Joyce Sequichie Hifler.
Counsel Oak books, Chicago Review Press.

CHAPTER TWO: THE CLIMB

Through traditional counselling, I learned the art of excavating, discovering the existence of my companion the Ego, the Animus/Anima[iv] and the unearthing of all things buried! What I truly benefited from was the recognition that traditional counselling is similar to archaeology, and this knowledge motivated a much deeper communication between myself and all life around me. It did not happen overnight though; it took many years to build my awareness and climb out of the hole I'd dug myself into!

SPEAK KINDLY TO YOUR SHADOW

As so often is the case with transformation, it began with a desire for change. For someone like me who harbored a lifetime of mistrust, relationships were always a challenge. Early in my life, somewhere near the end of the 70's, I was a single parent yet again! It was around this time that I found myself feeling a need to lighten my load, so I remarried for the third time. At the urging of my new husband Larry, I gave up my current job with the Federal Government along with what felt like a modicum of security. With the combination of a new husband, a new home, and a new school for the kids, the prospect of not working for the first time in a long time seemed the ideal decision for making life easier on all of us. What comes to mind as I record this is a Mr. Muscle Oven Cleaner commercial that was on television back then (1977): *"Be a good cook," Mother said, "and you'll get a man." What did I get? 25 years with my head stuck in a dirty oven!* I can remember laughing till I cried, every time that commercial came on! Why? What was so funny? Deep down, did I recognize a truth, one that contained the true humour of the ages?

Well, so much for the romantic notion of marital bliss and a leisurely life at home with my family; one month after my decision to stay home, I received a call about a job posted at the Community College nearby. Jannette Belanger, a childhood friend, was a student there, and upon reading the job description, she was convinced it was written for my skill set. And so, the rest is history. An exciting challenge was presented, and by my very nature, I was unable to decline.

During the 80's, I happily enjoyed a traditional career at Centennial College in Toronto. It was a new career, a new marriage and a new start for the kids and I. What could be better? At least that's what I told myself. But what was the reality? Hard work that kept me busy and often worn to a frazzle. Juggling the determination to attend night school with my family's need for my time and energy! Climbing by design to a more prestigious position and a higher income, but for what? Chaos and dysfunction plagued my good intentions for all of us to enjoy each other and our life together. This time in my life reminds me of the song "Send in the Clowns" by Judy Collins: *But where are the clowns / Send in the Clowns / Don't bother, they're here.*

At the college, in my new capacity as Director of Testing, I was designing, creating and managing College Testing Centers at several campuses. Initially, my work at the provincial level of government proved to be a significant challenge, but my previously extensive and diverse employment with the Federal Government provided the much-needed skills to successfully execute my provincial mandate.

The following years were exciting and I accomplished much by way of a professional career. Finally, being able to attend night school, I benefited from numerous college courses. I also acted upon my desire to serve others by training and studying with the College Union. Like my step-father, Alex Power, one of the original founders of the Letter Carriers Union of Canada (Roger Decarie, President & Alex Power, Vice-President of the National Letter Carriers Union of Canada, 1965), I felt an innate responsibility toward protecting and improving the working conditions for my coworkers and students alike! Through this commitment, I developed wonderful relationships that would last a lifetime…*two in particular are Rick Davis, and my bestie, Denise Andrews.*

No life could have been fuller than mine, yet again, after seven[v] productive years, I was questioning things. I found myself reading books by Dr. Wayne Dyer, Dan Millman, Brooke Medicine Shield, Judith Durick, Gary Zukav and Neale Donald Walsh just to name a few. Restlessness grew and so did the disruptions in my life! One after another, seemingly out of my control, children and husband challenges were mounting daily! The desire to assist students and staff by fighting the battles on their behalf wore thin to the point of exhaustion. Work simply lost its glow.

In the end, restlessness gave way to panic. Fight mode turned to flight, and the landscape of emotional depletion formed one of survival and self-preservation! *Who the hell was I? How did I get here? I must be an imposter! It's just a matter of time till I'm discovered for the fraud that I really am! Run, run as fast and as far as you can. Outrun your demons and your self-imposed prison! Don't stop long enough to look back; you have no idea what is chasing you, trying to catch up! Fear of what is behind you will be your salvation. Move, just keep moving at any and all cost...*and running is what I did. I left the security of an excellent career. I quit my job and eventually my marriage, and began a series of businesses that required me to relocate to other provinces and the United States.

SHIT! I bought the complete bill of goods, running like an untethered horse, without sense, without course, without direction. But damn it, I was free! In the absence of my prison, I couldn't help but wonder what aspect of my personality had been dictating the choices for my life during all that time. How could I have been so unconsciously involved in making those decisions?

The answer was simpler than I could ever have imagined, but nonetheless still a shocking realization; **it was simply due to my *lack of self-love.***

THE COCOON OF DEFIANCE

My lack of self-love must have come from somewhere, and if psychology taught me anything, it was that our programming starts early on in life, in childhood.

For most of my life, I existed in a cocoon of defiance, but where did it generate from? Was it a voice deep inside that was unbending and immovable? *"I may have to be here, but I don't have to like it."* Like *what*, exactly?

Perhaps this defiant stance originated during the time my sisters and I were boarded at a house on Gerrard Street in Toronto. We arrived with our mother and our suitcases in tow. The woman of the house greeted us warmly and led us all into the living room where she introduced us to her 9-year-old daughter and a very shy, 4-year-old boy, named Lucky. Jeanette, my older sister, remembered all these details and the fact that there was a husband as well.

Our new caregiver made us feel very welcome and talked about all the fun we would have, living with her family. Soon it was bedtime. Mom picked up my younger sister

Karon, and followed the woman upstairs. Jeanette and I followed close behind. When we arrived at the bedroom there was a crib for Karon and beds for Jeanette and I to sleep in. Mom helped us unpack our pajamas because it was bedtime. She kissed us all and said goodnight. Then she left.

The next morning the woman who had been so kind the night before, woke us up early. She told us to take off our pajamas and directed Jeanette to pick up Karon before marching us down stairs in our underwear! Not to the main floor, but all the way down to the basement.

The first thing we were greeted by were bunk beds lining the walls, and a toilet, standing in the open room. There, in a cold unfinished basement sat eight other children, two of which were as young as our Karon.

We were told to take something to wear from a large pile of clothing on the floor. Then directed to sit down at a table with benches, and eat our breakfast. While Jeanette tried to eat the cornmeal gruel that was in her bowl she began to gag as if to throw-up. The woman became cross and told Jeanette that she had better swallow every bit of it, or else!

My baby sister Karon cried all the time; she was hungry and missed our mother. She also wet the bed, which was perfectly understandable considering her young age. But the woman who kept us got very angry with her, as did some of the other children. I don't remember standing up for her…maybe I was just too young. I do know that I spent the rest of my childhood, my life in fact, doing so, even if inconsistently!

Sometimes, Jeanette and another girl named Linda would sneak upstairs when the family was asleep. Both girls had watched the lady put bread in a drawer of the stove. The two of them only risked taking one slice each for fear that the bread would be missed! My sister Jeanette still carries guilt that she and the other girl ate the food they stole and didn't share with the rest of us. I would imagine even more traumatic for Jeanette, was the survivor's guilt at being the first child mom rescued from that terrible place! Although she was happy and relieved when mom came to take her away, knowing that her younger sisters were being left to survive in horrible conditions would haunt her psyche. My, my, my…what burdens shape innocence.

I have little memory of the other children living in the basement with Karon and I. However, my sister Jeanette, being that much older than us, remembers them well. Subsequently, as adults, my sisters and I have discussed the actions of the woman who kept us. The woman we stayed with had a family of her own. My older sister remembers playing outside with her kids and thinking they were nice. However, my baby sister Karon, myself, and the other younger children were never allowed out of the basement to play, or for any other reason, with the exception of occasional visits with our mother that were thoroughly monitored.

My sister describes our visits with mom as being carefully orchestrated by the woman who looked after us, making sure to dress us up nicely in our clothes. Cute little smock style dresses that mom had made for us, hand embroidered across the top. Little white socks and shoes. Freshly washed faces and well-groomed hair; the picture of well-being. Karon clung to our mother during the entire visit while I defiantly kept myself thoroughly distanced.

Collectively, my sisters and I have come to suspect that the caregiver kept us out of sight so the neighbours did not know we were there. By dealing with our presence in this manner, she could keep us away from prying eyes and the need to declare us as income. Whatever the reason, 11 children were left traumatized and their lives shaped accordingly from living with the memories of that house on Gerrard Street.

We were fed regularly, but experienced constant hunger, which reminds me of a quote by Mother Teresea: "The hunger for love is far greater than hunger for food." In reflection, I'm now able to see how the little girl I was back then, came to mistrust adults, pure and simple. Her perception of the world was directly tainted by harsh experiences. Especially the memory of trudging down the stairs to that unfriendly basement; an overcrowded children's den!

At my editor's suggestion I have placed these cathartic memories on paper. It provided a glimpse into myself as that little girl. She truly wanted to be reunited with her mother and sisters. However, there was no way she could trust or accept any future adult mischief. Within her limited understanding of the world, it would not be safe to. I imagine this is where my defiance was born as a defense mechanism. As long as she was deciding to defy, she held a sense of power!

SPEAK KINDLY TO YOUR SHADOW

After my father divorced our mother, she began dating the man that was to become our future stepfather. She eventually found the courage to tell him she had a daughter. The rationale for revealing just one daughter, we can only assume, was due to a previous relationship that ended abruptly when our mother chose to be honest and admitted having three children!

With our future stepfather, the revelation of a little girl still living in care was unacceptable. This child deserved to be reunited with her mother. He then proposed moving in together, making it possible for her to remove her daughter from care. My older sister Jeanette liked him well enough, and was most grateful to be living with mom again. Trips to Centre Island, a Davy Crocket hat, and an introduction to libraries and books that would shape her love of reading and learning, were just a few examples of this man's generosity. The three of them got along well.

After being securely married, my mother informed her new husband of the existence of two more children! I am better able now, as a mother myself, to recognize the courage and bravery of this woman, my mother, always living in fear and apprehension for herself and her children, especially when dating a new man. Like Swiss psychologist Carl Jung once said, "The meeting of two personalities is like the contact of two chemical substances: if there is any reaction, both are transformed." Our new stepfather now had to face reality; there were two more children and they were still living in care! We girls have had many discussions over the years, and have come to believe that this early deception by our mother may well explain, in part, why our Scottish step-father became such a jealous, angry, and often brutal man after finding out about our mother's lie of omission.

Whatever else this man was, he was a man of principle. He saw it as his duty to provide a home for his wife and her children. These little girls needed to be removed from care and he would make sure this happened. After my mother and stepfather collected Karon to live with them and Jeanette, arrangements were made to collect me from yet another house, where I had recently been relocated to.

And so, I was the last to be retrieved. I still coddle the memory of marching up those stairs on Knox Ave in total defiance thinking to myself, "I may have to be here but I don't have to like it!" Defiant or not, the reality was that all three of us girls were finally reunited with our mother and living together under the same roof with a new stepfather. We were a family again!

However, this was a false bravado that had to end eventually. Underneath it all, my anger and defiance swarmed, but this needed to subside too if there was any chance for me to become familiar with love. This would only be possible through intimacy with myself. Over time, I came to question my general lack of intimacy in life, even with God during prayer and meditation where I sought access to God through the animals, Mother Earth and all my relations! Why couldn't I find that deep and loving connection, that intimacy, even amidst something as sacred as prayer?

MY 'NOT ENOUGHNESS'

Eventually I realized that by loving myself and others with *conditions*, love is not even present.

Every expression I made consciously or otherwise had a motive. *Can my needs be met? Will I be safe? Will I receive the sense of self-worth I require? Will I feel valued? Will I experience being whole and complete? Will I be enough? Will my expression of love make me happy?* These are fair questions that should be asked.

However, I asked these questions of others, even though they could not possibly provide the answers. Society taught me to reach outward, not inward! Culturally, I have felt forced to doubt anything that is 'I' centred, and this programming was very thorough. Look anywhere for satisfaction, answers, and guidance—anywhere but within!

Realizing this has been the catalyst for recognizing the need to reframe my perception of the world and my place in it. Now when I love, I love! Free of judgement and emotion, without rhyme or reason—because love is natural and organic. Like God, it just is. God is love and love is God expressed. *This was to be realized through the gift of Reframing!*

The answers exist and always have. Even illness, for which I have much personal experience, sheds light. Once I understood that I was raised and indoctrinated into a belief system where sickness was normal and all things are separate and either good and bad, healthy and unhealthy, right and wrong, pleasant and unpleasant, happy and sad, I came to realize that I would never find peace there. As long as I continued any attempts to fit in, to be accepted and understood, I would spend my entire life struggling. Frustration and an inability to belong would be my stead.

Truly, the only option was to follow the path of least resistance, but I didn't know what that path looked like. I began seeking answers from many well-informed, wise and accomplished people. Their path served them and their journey well, however, it seemed I was unable to effectively adapt their knowledge into my own life; I was still frustrated and not at peace with myself!

Then came the real judgments of my not enoughness, my worthlessness, my inability to receive genuine value and transformation from those who wore the badges. These wonderful accomplished people graciously shared the way, the truth, the light—yet there I was, sitting on my arse and scratching my head. Or is it the other way round? I'm reminded of that British expression "some mothers do 'ave 'em."[vi] Why oh why could I not get it…whatever *it* was?

My friend Patricia Saville and I would walk the boardwalk in the Toronto Beaches for hours, talking, laughing, hashing things out, always seeking answers while acknowledging our determination to be hit upside the head by the proverbial two by four! We would make fun of ourselves by saying, "Knowing our luck, the *aha moment* or the light bulb switching on will happen just as we take our last breath!" This very necessary emergence of humour would continue to surface and magically thread its gift of colouring my path with light and joy while filling it with awe and wonder.

Fortunately, through much determination, humour and friendship like that which Patricia and I shared, profound and transformative experiences began to surface in my life. Finally shedding light on a path forward. My way of being began to change before my eyes.

AWAKENED BY ANGELS

Fortunately for myself, the angels entered my journey.

When this experience materialized in my life, it reframed my understanding of the world and my place in it. I never really questioned their introduction into my life, or their offering of a safe place, a sacred and loving space for God and I to commune. What I have come to recognize is that I never perceived the angels to be anything other than angels. With them, I was not being manipulated by adults, but rather conversing with the divine.

Dearest St. Francis Xavier was to be the angel that awakened me to the unlimited lessons of vision. His commitment to getting my attention in a rather unorthodox manner was brilliant and perfect. He was unafraid to reach out to me through humour and recognized my propensity for laughter.

One such experience must be the billboard! Yes, the same billboard story from my book *Angels Do The Darndest Things.* It happens while I'm driving along Vancouver's King Edward Boulevard. I'm dazzled! Or maybe just dazed? The sun, warming the ocean breeze wafting through my open window is courted by music from the radio, *"Riding along in my automobile…"* (Chuck Berry, "No Place to Go"). And just as I'm about to reach the traffic lights at Arbutus…I see it! I can't quite believe it, but I really do see it.

A giant billboard! Right there in the middle of the old railway plot. When did they put that up? And what's with the monk? It reads: St. Francis Xavier. Who? The only Xavier I know of is the Spanish musician and bandleader Xavier Cugat. Oh, darn! The lights turn green, and I need to turn! I continue my drive to my friend's house, knowing I'm just minutes away from Maple Street, my intended destination. Fortunately, my friend is an excellent teacher and has lived in Vancouver most of her adult life. If anyone knows when and why the billboard was put up, she will.

The first words out of my mouth when I walk through her door are, "Hi there, do you know who St. Francis Xavier is?"

"Who?" she asks

"Some guy who I think is a monk," I replied, "and is named St. Francis Xavier?"

"The name does sound familiar, but I'm not sure. Perhaps the computer at the library would be helpful?" she offers.

"No, if you don't know who he is, I'll call my sister back east. She seems to be doing a lot of research papers these days for her university courses. I'll see what she can turn up."

"Why this particular monk and why now?" asks my friend.

"Well, I'm just curious. I mean till today, I never noticed that giant billboard at King

Edward and Arbutus. And since the only thing on the sign was the picture of a monk with the name St. Francis Xavier…I thought you of all people would know what it's about. Didn't you tell me that you went to a Catholic girl's school in Ireland?"

"Hold on a minute! You're telling me there's a billboard on the old railway property at the corner of Arbutus?" my friend asks in astonishment.

My friend was even more surprised than me to hear about this billboard, and at a total loss as to its new development in her neighbourhood.

The following day, she came by my place to collect my left-handed golf clubs as she had secured a buyer for them and was to deliver the clubs in person. When she arrived at my place that morning, she was not very happy! It turns out that my good friend went out of her way to drive by the new billboard at King Edward and Arbutus.

Imagine if you will, her consternation at finding no such sign! The old, abandoned railway plot was exactly as it had been for years. Nothing on it. Zero. Zilch. Nada.

"Ridiculous, that's absolutely ridiculous!" I replied indignantly. "You drive, I'm coming with you. We'll drive over together. It has to be there…I couldn't possibly imagine a giant billboard!"

But when we arrived, there was no billboard. No sign. The old, abandoned railway plot was as overgrown and unattended as ever. I thought to myself—it's finally happened; I've gone round the bend. I'm beginning to see things that aren't there.

I shake my head in absolute dismay all the way back home. My friend has now calmed down and is doing her best to console me. The next day I regrouped and called my sister back east, to investigate the matter further. Her research provided some rather interesting information.

SPEAK KINDLY TO YOUR SHADOW

Saint Francis Xavier[vii], born 1506 and died 1552, was one of the seven people who in 1534 at Montmartre, founded the society of Jesus: Order of the Jesuits. What I truly gleaned through Xavier's decision to introduce himself by way of the billboard was twofold. First, was the knowledge that this Saint perceived Jesus in a way that was foreign to me, leaving me to research and acquire new information that provided a much-expanded version of my previously limited perception of Jesus! And second, the billboard introduction clearly demonstrated Xavier's desire to teach me about vision through the gift of humour. This experience taught me how to trust and laugh at myself—a rare kindness indeed.

Another of my introductions to true love and humour was through the Angel Ophilius. During a number of weekend workshops with a wonderful teacher by the name of Linda Sedesky, author of *Gathering Our Divinity* (Trafford Publishing, 2000), I was one of a group of seven people who participated in her classes on Energy & Angels. It was at this time that I was introduced to Elsie Poloquin and the magnificent Angel Dolls that she constructed. The following story is also found in my book, *Angels Do The Darndest Things.*

My friend Elsie presented the teacher, Linda, with an Angel Doll figure she had made for her. Linda replied, "Oh, that's so nice Elsie, thank you." Then she released a gasp and said, "This is the angel Ophilious!"

When Linda let out a gasp, so too did I, because I was totally convinced that I knew this angel as well. I remarked that the angel had shown himself to me in the weeks *before* the workshop, and in the strangest possible way.

I was sitting in the living room of my friend (the same one who lived near the billboard) having a conversation, when suddenly I found myself *energetically* sitting in the back of a stretch limousine. In the front seat, the driver was all dressed up in his limousine livery, with white wiry hair sticking out beneath his cap. Slowly turning round his eyes met mine, blue and sparkling like the Ionian Sea, alive and dancing with unbridled merriment! A smile that graduated from mischievous to infectious, holding me captive. I couldn't help myself; I started laughing! In fact, I was still laughing when I realized my friend was yelling at me, trying to get my attention.

I told Linda and Elsie this story. Undeniably, it was clear that both Linda and I had previously had exposure to the Angel Ophilius, for she too recounted an experience like mine. Through our willingness to share our personal experience of this angel, we affirmed for Elsie that she was right to trust her guidance and blessed to have been personally guided by Angel Ophilius in making his image manifest in the world through the creation of her Angel Doll.

Over the years, the angels assisted in my personal development by removing my head from the equation, setting my heart free to invite all I desired into my life. Through the organ of my heart, my soul broke away, untethered and boundless. It rallied my courage and strengthened my resolve to not only be here, *but to like it.*

THE SWEAT LODGE EXPERIENCE

On a visit to Vancouver in 1992 to spend Christmas with my son Rob, my niece Diane Elliot, invited me to participate in a Sweat Lodge ceremony at a Native Reservation. Having no knowledge of what a sweat lodge was but always up for a new experience, I agreed and asked how to dress for the occasion.

Upon hearing about my invitation, Rob, who is a ferocious reader, shared his limited knowledge of what was expected of me as a participant. With his contribution of tobacco, my long shirt, and a towel tucked snugly in a travel bag, I felt prepared. My niece and her partner Bill picked me up and drove us to the reserve. Bill was reticent in sharing knowledge of the Sweat Lodge with us; it made for a quiet car ride. In retrospect, I understand and applaud his discretion.

The ceremony was a Warrior's Sweat where grandfather rocks were heated carefully in an open fire and carried sacredly into the lodge[viii]. More rocks were added after each round until all the grandfathers were together. There were four rounds in the ceremony, with a break after each round. The Medicine Man 'Woody', who would go on to become *my* Medicine Teacher, was most insightful and shared many teachings.

During the second of four rounds, I had an out-of-body experience—literally! I previously had little knowledge or understanding of what was taking place during the sweat. However, as it was going on, I actually observed my physical body lying on the cedar bows, which covered the floor of the lodge. Steadily, I rose above my body, above the lodge and the fire-keeper. It was uncomplicated. With curiosity and delight I watched the fire and the rising sparks as I moved easily above them. Soon I was a part of the night sky with the stars, beaming alongside them.

Then—I was back in my body! Something cool and wet and smelling of cedar was being gently feathered over my entire body, and I heard someone say, "All my relations, the door."

As we left the sweat lodge at the conclusion of the second round, and returned to the building (a home) where we waited between rounds to stay out of the snow and cold, I felt light, empty and more expansive! I shared my incredible experience with the others. Woody, the Medicine Man was not without knowledge of it. He explained that he witnessed my soul leaving my body and knew when it was timely for my soul to return. I woke to the swishing of the cool and wet cedar bow as it was his way of preparing the body for the safe return of my soul.

In this experience, fire taught me to acknowledge the fire within, and assisted me in recognizing that spontaneity for living was dependent on my willingness to support my passion in life. The ability to create adventure and excitement comes from the willingness to give myself pleasure and joy. This began a true journey of discovery with the teachings of the Medicine Wheel and knowledge of my relationship with Mother Earth and All My Relations.

Through the Indigenous pathway, I was led to the people and connections that would propel me toward an understanding of Oneness, the truth of Wholeness that I was in search of. These people shared a collective commitment to walking the Red Road[ix] of our Ancestors in a good way, with an innate desire to share this journey with anyone who is guided to them.

My teachers came simply, if not always quietly. My first Medicine Man, Woody, who I believe is from the Tequitage Nation, provided my first experience of a sweat lodge. Workshops in Seattle with Rumi, who is referenced in the book and movie titled *The Secret*. Studies with Rubin, a shaman from Peru. Teachings from Leonard Crow Dog, a Sioux Warrior and studies with his niece Heather from the Dakota Sioux Nation. My shared friendship and teachings with Beverly Jones, from the Ojibway Territories who I was blessed to attend sweat lodges, healing and sharing circles, and the first reconciliation ceremony in Fort Alexander in 1997. I was privileged to work with Bev on Phil Fontain's campaign to become Grand Chief in Vancouver, B.C. I met many Medicine Teachers, like Nowell and fire keeper Norman, who held the space for my Vision Quest on

SPEAK KINDLY TO YOUR SHADOW

Bowen Island in 1995. Through my exposure to these amazing individuals, I have come to recognize and accept that every one of these experiences have been guided.

Now, my Shadow speaks clearly: "It is time."

My perception of the world was changing.

The paramount importance of logic and analytical skills was diminishing.

I was awakening inside of my dreamtime reality through an altered state of consciousness…

SANDRA ANNE DAVIS

"The world is but a canvas to our imaginations. Dreams are the touchstones of our characters."

—*HENRY DAVID THOREAU*

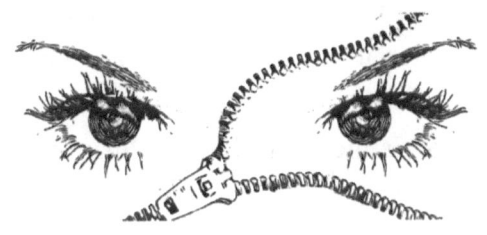

CHAPTER THREE: THE VISION QUEST

My experience of questing is that of a metaphysical journey towards a quiet understanding that is not accessible through everyday mental action or general processes of acquiring knowledge and understanding through thought, experience, and the senses. This quiet understanding could only be accessed through metaphysical means such as dreaming, meditative altered states, and higher guidance.

In fact, long before awareness in conscious form materialized in my life as a child, I was receiving shamanic guidance. *The Sacred Path Cards* by Jamie Sams describe Shamanism as: "the ability to commune with spirits dwelling on all levels of Creation. When a person has this ability from an early age, it can be severely misunderstood. The natural shaman has usually had one or more major traumas between the ages of one and seven [which was indeed my experience]. These traumatic events cause a tear in the embryonic ego matrix that destroys the boundaries of the child…If an imbalance exists within her ego matrix that has not been uncovered, the shaman has a responsibility to search for the origin of fragmentation. Always the search is in pursuit of wholeness…nothing less than union and reunion with the divine." This aligns nicely with another quote from *The Book of Runes* about wholeness and reunion with the divine which says: "This way of thinking and Being integrates new energies and permits us to flow into wholeness, which is the ultimate goal of the Spiritual Warrior."

I didn't know it at the time, but the Shamanic guidance I received as a child was just preparation for accessing knowledge through the art of questing! This would serve me throughout my life. Quests, I might add that were often unconscious. Spirit was firm and unrelenting in its determination to direct my path through vision! What follows is an account of several of the visions I received that relate to turning points in my life. My first sweat lodge experience offered an out of body experience that introduced me to the reality of the illusion of separation. It was here that I first experienced my true connection to everything!

The gift of a Native Vision Quest on Bowen Island in 1995 was to offer four days on the mountain. Here the space was held and protected in a sacred way by Medicine man Nowell and firekeeper Norman. Details of this and other sacred ceremonies are to remain with me. However, I have chosen to provide an account of some of my visions to provide context from personal experience.

THE BOY IN THE WHITE DRESS

Boom, boom, boom, boom….boom, boom, boom….boom, boom, boom, boom….boom, boom, boom….the beating drum tells me that it's time to dream!

I'm dreaming[x] of a house filled with women. We are all in the living room, some of us listening, others talking. I'm standing against the frame of an open door leading from one of the other rooms to this one. There are women all over the room, sitting on chairs, couches, ottomans and even on the floor. Others are leaning against walls, door frames and furniture. All of these women seem very comfortable and a little excited; it is good energy everywhere.

The doorbell rings and two women arrive. One is much older than me, and the other is a younger woman carrying a baby in her arms. I leave them to be taken care of, anticipating that I'll introduce myself to them after they're settled. When I see my opportunity, I walk over to meet the older woman while she is talking to her grandson, the baby, who's now having his coat removed.

"Hello," I say, "I have been looking forward to meeting you." I can't help but notice how nice her red[xi] short-sleeved sweater looks with her white hair.

As the older woman acknowledges my greeting, she studies me with a look that is curious and warm. "Yes, well," she says and we enter into dialogue.

We start to talk about an article that I've written. She wants to know who the article is for and how I came to write it. I tell her that possibly it would be best to receive the article in its original context, when the book is published.

"The book!" she says. "Whose book?"

"My book," I say, "which should be published soon."

"Oh, I see!" says the woman. "Yes, well we shall see, if it should be published."

"Oh, it will be, and this is going to happen in April." I state this firmly and with more conviction than I ever remember feeling since the inception of my book.

Later, when she and her companion and grandson are preparing to leave, I come to say goodbye and share my pleasure at meeting her. She looks straight into my eyes once again before speaking.

"I recognized you while walking up the path to the front door. I saw you through the large window. You stood apart from the other women in posture and composure. The other women were excited, fuzzy and prickly. You, however, were calm and grounded."

Without warning, she firmly nudges her female companion to hold out the baby boy for me to take. As she holds the boy with outstretched arms, I notice he's wearing a white dress and little white socks and shoes.

He begins to squirm as I reach out to accept him and looks at me with fear and apprehension. I immediately pull back and smile at the child. I, too, look straight into his face and say, "You must feel very uncomfortable with all these women around you. I do not want to add to your discomfort so please do not worry dear. You can stay right there in your mother's arms where you feel safe." I also tell him that if or when he wants to talk to me, he is always welcome to, because I like to spend time talking and listening to children.

Soon the three of them are walking down the path toward a waiting car and it's then that

I notice my reflection. I'm wearing the same red short-sleeved sweater as the older woman. As they reach the car, the little boy turns in his mother's arms and holds up something for me to see. I strain to see what it is. He yells out "Twee!" and holds it up over his mother's shoulder.

As the older woman opens the car door to allow mother and baby to get into the vehicle, the little boy squeals and squirms free. He runs back to me calling out, "Twee!" I'm already walking swiftly toward him and as I approach, it looks as though what he is holding is a very thin smooth tree branch, a twig, with nothing left on it. "Twee!" he says again, and then I understand.

"Oh yes dear! You are absolutely right; this is part of the big tree over there." I accept the branch, taking his little hand and leading him over to the big beautiful tree to my right, his left[xii].

SPEAK KINDLY TO YOUR SHADOW

It's a very large cedar tree with a natural sitting area on the ground, created by its soft fallen branches. Together, as I talk and the boy listens, we sit down on the soft bed of cedar boughs and I begin to tell him the story about trees and their relationship to him and I...

THE LITTLE TREE

Once upon a time there was a very little tree. He was lonely and wanted very much to experience companionship. One day, a little girl came by and stopped right in front of the tree, admiring its beauty and strength. She saw the little tree in perspective of its environment. It was truly very tiny in comparison to all the other elements—the power of the wind, the raging of the sea, the brilliant blinding rays of the sun; this little tree was truly a microcosm in a macrocosm!

Suddenly, the little girl began to cry. She sat down on the ground, just like you and I are doing now, and she wept and wept and wept…just as I am doing now!

She cried and she wept so much that the ground around her began to fill up with water and formed a pond. This little tree was now standing beside a beautiful clear pond. And as she continued to cry and weep, the birds and the animals which lived much farther away in the deepest parts of the forest came out to see what all the ruckus was about—after all, they had never heard a girl crying before!

The little tree suddenly had all kinds of companions. He had the little girl, the pond, the birds and all the other animals. When the little girl finally stopped crying and raised her head, she too discovered the animals and realized she was sitting in the middle of a pond! She was very surprised and immediately waded to the shore, to dry ground. She was about to walk over and sit underneath the little tree when the tree spoke to her.

SPEAK KINDLY TO YOUR SHADOW

"Little girl, what you need most right now is warmth. You are still wet from the water[xiii], your tears. The brilliance of the sun's[xiv] rays are where you can find the most warmth. I would love nothing more than to have you sit here with me, but I'm afraid you might get cold and sick, and then leave. You see, that has been my experience with little girls and boys who get sick; they always go away!"

So, the little girl got up and ran off to an open field. She laid down in the soft grass and spread out her arms and legs so that the sun's rays could warm her body all over. It felt wonderful, the same way she'd felt when she recognized the beauty and strength of the little tree. She began to weep once again. She wept and wept and wept. She quite literally cried herself a river. Before too long, the current began moving the little girl *gently down the stream…merrily, merrily, merrily, merrily, life is but a dream…* flowing around rocks and trees and bushes

Then rather unexpectedly, she began to hear a waterfall. She felt its vibration in the current! Her heart began to race, fear and apprehension flooding her veins. Instinctively she began to struggle, to fight the currents carrying her along.

The very flow that had been so gentle at first, now became the enemy. The harder she struggled the more difficult it became to keep her head above water. Finally, in one last fated attempt to save herself, she reached out and grabbed the branch of a tree.

With what felt like no effort at all, the tree plucked the little girl out of the fast-moving current of the river and cradled her in its arms. With the power of the wind, the tree was able to rock the little girl, making her feel safe once again. She stayed cradled in the safety and warmth that she had now come to know quite personally. She stayed there for a very long time

SPEAK KINDLY TO YOUR SHADOW

One day as she was being gently rocked, back and forth, back and forth, a bird came to her and landed softly on the bough she was on. He sang the sweetest song she had ever heard. His singing made her feel as wonderful as she had when she first recognized the beauty and strength of the little tree. She began to weep. She wept and wept and wept. Before too long, her tears were flowing over the countryside, through pastures, over hill tops and down into the valleys below, until she had undoubtedly created a sea of tears; that's why the ocean's water is salty like a woman's tears!

Then the tears stopped.

Soon, the power of the wind was no more.

The sun's rays began to diminish. The warmth was gone.

The tree was still, motionless, almost as if it were holding its breath, waiting—but for what?

The little girl was very confused, very frightened.

What was it that she was beginning to feel?

It began with a sense of irritation; things just weren't what she had been told or led to believe her whole life.

Then, she was able to discern between half-truths and outright lies! What was really going on? So much negativity everywhere!

No room for *truth*, for *growth*, for *integrity*!

No hope of restoring beauty and strength like that which she had recognized in the little tree!

Anger—flushing, fuming, rage, and soon the sea itself responded with crashing waves large enough to wash the planet and cleanse it of all its lies, leaving only that which is *truth*.

Truth lives in the trees and the trees know all of the stories about girls and boys and the stories about trees.

The *truth*, *growth* and *integrity* necessary for the existence of current and future generations is kept alive in the trees. It is from their leaves, their flowers, and their fruit that the knowledge of humankind lives on and is transmuted.

THE CAVE FIRE

I've awoken from this dream, only to find myself standing on the ledge of a rockface.

It is quite large and very flat. As I stand here admiring the incredible view, I begin to feel something watching me. Those green eyes are so intense! I never realized before that cougars have green eyes. Suddenly the wild cat pounces and begins to tear me apart. I'm aware of what is taking place, but I feel no pain.

Now I'm lying naked in a field and soldiers are cutting out my vulva and cutting off my breasts to make pouches. Again, no pain. In an instant, I'm no longer the woman on the ground; I'm one of the soldiers doing the cutting. Blood, red with rage and the stench of tearing flesh.

Now I'm vomiting…

The next thing I know, I'm lying beside a fire inside a cave. There is an old woman there, stitching me back together. She has a very large needle, fashioned from the tooth of a grizzly bear. Patiently she sews, yet still I feel no pain.

Suddenly I hear the sharp cry of an eagle! Then I see it; a large, very muscular cougar, with fur that glistens in the sunlight. As our eyes meet, a soft and gentle feeling washes over my entire body. His deep guttural purrs invade.

I can feel the warmth of the fire now. The old woman smiles down on me and I know that I've been put back together. Slowly and deliberately, I rise as her eyes direct me to the opening of the cave. I step out into the sunshine and deeply inhale the fresh mountain air.

Now there is a man's face, tender and kind, looking deep into my eyes. I turn my head in search of the gentleness in his voice. I feel life returning to my veins. Yes! I heard him coming, the beating drum spoke to me of his arrival. I've never known this kind of love…it's calling me back.

Boom, Boom, Boom…Boom, Boom, Boom
Boom, Boom, Boom…Boom, Boom, Boom….

MEDICINE MAN SHARING CIRCLE

Shortly after my Vision Quest, I attended one of many Sharing Circles in Vancouver. This was to be a special evening with a Medicine Man from New Zealand. At the time, he was travelling the world sharing his teachings, in particular the sacredness of whale medicine.

In the book *Medicine Cards* by Jamie Sams & David Carson, they introduce whale medicine as: *"Whale is very much like a swimming library. Whale carries the history of Mother Earth and is said to have been placed here by the Ancients from the dog star, Sirius. Biologists say that Whale is a mammal, and very possibly lived on land millions of years ago. In tribal legends, the Whale's move into the ocean happened when the Earth shifted and Lemuria, the Motherland, went below the waves."*

The Medicine Man from New Zealand believed in Whale as a keeper of the knowledge, and he and his tribe respect and honour this medicine in a very special way. When the tribe recognizes early potential in a child, they will take that child under their collective care and nurture the child's spiritual and physical development.

Once the child has reached their spiritual maturity and is ready for their final initiation, the child is rowed out to sea and released into the ocean to join Whale, as their apprentice. When and if Whale shows up for the child, the child will serve an apprenticeship with the whales until the whales have shared the extent of their knowledge with the child. In honour of these teachings, the child will return to the tribe and educate the people.

Whale…
Of mighty oceans,
You have seen it all.
Teach me how to hear your words,
And how to understand,
The very roots of history,
Of where our world began

(Whale meaning, *Medicine Cards: The Discovery of Power Through the Ways of Animals,* pg. 201 Jamie Sams & David Carson, 1999).

The day of the Sharing Circle with this New Zealand Medicine Man, a strong feeling surfaced within me—my 6-year-old niece Lyndsay Elliot was to accompany me. This quiet voice speaking from deep within me was not completely foreign; there was a familiarity to it. The more I heeded this voice in my life, the more grounded and centred I became.

And so, I brought my niece with me. Near the completion of the circle, each participant walked around a Sharing Blanket, upon which lay many different gifts. Participants were meant to choose a gift that spoke to them. My niece was excited by the gift she had chosen. She whispered to me that she had wanted the seashell from when she first spotted it on the blanket!

As I followed her around the sacred blanket, it became evident that all the gifts were taken. I personally had never experienced this before. Lyndsay, with gift in hand, and myself, returned to our sitting place in the circle. Settling down on the floor, Norm, the fire keeper from my first vision quest on Bowen Island in B.C. appeared behind me. He quietly whispered that he had something for me at the close of the circle.

SPEAK KINDLY TO YOUR SHADOW

When the ceremony ended, Lyndsay held her beautiful seashell gift to my ear so I could hear the sound of the ocean! As the circle broke up, Norm appeared beside me. I was very glad to see him again. He explained that he had been guided to attend this evening and to bring the gift he had for me. As I accepted his gift, tears of joy and gratitude washed over me. Of course, there was no gift left on the blanket for me; a very specific gift from Spirit was my stead.

Through tears of gratitude rolling freely down my cheeks, I studied the beautiful, yet tiny medicine bag Norm had just given me. It was made from deer skin and hung on a string so that I could wear it around my neck. According to my Medicine Cards, deer represent gentleness[xv]. Beaded carefully in the centre of the deer skin bag was a red strawberry. Red represents the root chakra and walking the Red Road, which means to deeply commit to living life in the best way possible—

with an intrinsic respect for others, oneself and the Creator. It is also worth noting that a strawberry[xvi] wears its seeds on the outside of its skin.

Norm smiled as he observed me and suggested I reach inside my little medicine bag. There I discovered a tiny amber stone. I have come to understand the meaning of amber and its significance to my life best through this explanation:

"Amber allows the body to heal itself by absorbing and transmuting negative energy into positive energy. It emits a sunny, bright and soothing energy which helps to calm nerves and to enliven the disposition. The different colours of amber may be used on the appropriate chakras to facilitate opening and cleansing. It is a stone dedicated to the connection of the conscious self to universal perfection. It also transmutes the energy of physical vitality toward the activation of unconditional love. Amber provides an energy to kindle the realization and subsequent response of choice, helping one to choose and to be chosen." (*Love Is in the Earth: A Kaleidoscope of Crystals* by Melody. Earth Love Pub House, 1995.)[xvii]

Amazing! I would like to take this moment to connect you back to Chapter One when I talked about governing oneself divinely through choice and responsibility, 'the ability to respond'. How incredibly significant for Norm to gift me this amber stone at that particular time in my life.

This Sharing Circle and my prior Vision Quest were the birth of 'vision' itself for me. From that point forward, I began to see life more clearly, and when you see things with more clarity, you can become more intentional.

My gift is the power of my intention; I have the power to decide what limits I am willing to cloak and those with which I am willing to engage. Everything is a choice! And the choices I make serve my journey, just as your choices serve your journey.

This combination of differing methodologies with the angels and the Medicine Wheel never seemed at odds or unusual to me at any time or in any way. But why would they? Their message of inclusiveness was never in dispute. Both were reflecting an internal landscape of clear and unwavering knowledge of my connection with everything, with God, governing oneself divinely. The angels and their extraordinary methodology for communication reinforced my subjective understanding of the Medicine Wheel and its teachings of a collective belief of illusion—of separateness! The knowledge from the Medicine Wheel that our lives are vibrations, continuously propelling us, helps me to better understand the nature of the Wheel of Life; the endless cycle of birth, death and rebirth, especially in Buddhism. The cyclical rotation of the wheel forces us to spiral to its core and back out again. Constant movement and progression erode what no longer serves us, while unearthing what is required to regain balance and experience peace.

There's no doubt that the angels and Medicine Wheel teachings reframed my entire life up to that point and continue to do so today. Who knows what your reframing will look like? Perhaps you are already undergoing it in your life, or in small ways throughout your days. I would now like to share with you some of the key elements of reframing that I have incorporated throughout my experiences.

SANDRA ANNE DAVIS

"It is only with the <u>heart</u> that one can see rightly; what is essential is invisible to the eye."
   —*Antoine de Saint-Exupéry, Le Petit Prince*

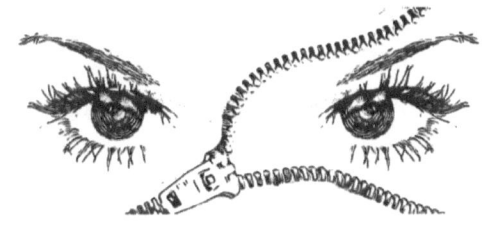

CHAPTER FOUR: THE ART OF REFRAMING THE DIVINE

THE GIFT OF MIRRORS

During my years as a Spiritual Counsellor, beginning as Director of the Wellness Center at Centennial and continuing through private practice at The Woman's Lodge, my clients and I have shared much. Through these amazing individuals, my understanding of gratitude was deeply developed. I evolved through our exchanges, just as they evolved, changing individually and collectively. Our gift to one another was the mirror of authenticity that we each provided, a reflection of truth that gave us courage and an understanding of our value and worth.

Through the use of mirrors, an unspoken covenant—to bear witness—was established. We all bear witness for each other because reflection is our inheritance and the way in which we divulge all that we have come to believe. Everything that keeps us distant from the truth, forges bars of steel. Trust is the component we need to penetrate the illusion of separation, because the nature of trust is organic, allowing each person to feel safe and seen! Through trust, beauty and strength can emerge. A separation no longer exists.

One of the best examples of this that I have experienced, is the relationship I have with my husband. Rick and I interpret what we see of the world through different lenses. We could become at odds with one another if either of us became reactionary. Instead, we both made a conscious effort to accept without judgement the other person and their right to choose what works for them as an individual, allowing these choices to go beyond our frail understanding! I would like to add here that this (our relationship, our marriage) was a successful collaboration in reframing—not tolerance (most of the time, ha ha!).

Relationships have taught me that when I do not trust the universe to function perfectly, it reciprocates. It always gives me what I believe, by providing mirrors. Often, these mirrors are darn uncomfortable! But through this discomfort I became familiar enough with what I *don't* want.

The interesting discovery of what I don't want provides a new clarity; a realization that my decisions, my choices, are not providing peace, but rather, disruption and even chaos. I also became aware of an arrogance evidenced in my exchanges—that I know my own needs better than Infinite Intelligence or God does. This is an independent ego, predetermining a misconception that I am separate from God!

Now, what exactly is Infinite Intelligence? I've always loved this definition of Infinite Intelligence:

"Intuition is Infinite Intelligence talking to us between our thoughts!"

(Phil Lauth, from *You Can Have It All* by Arnold Patent pg 37)

To deny Infinite Intelligence is to deny our own intuition and keep us separate from God. Realizing that this belief in separation does not serve me, my highest good, or the highest good of others, and trusting that God is the same energy of love that I am, is *key* to surrendering, just as this prayer for the soul's journey says: "*I will to will Thy Will*" *(The Book of Runes*, page 132, Ralph H. St. Martin's Press, New York.)* Letting go of the illusion of separation requires *patience,* not practice. When I choose to remain cognizant of the collective perception of being less than God, and agree to take ownership of the way I emanate this reflection into the world, then I must also be willing to exercise compassion for myself.

This does not need to be a challenge if I remember that compassion is the natural expression of Infinite Intelligence! Put another way—if I'm unable to see or accept my own magnificence as a mirror of Infinite Intelligence, of God, how will I ever be able to see and accept the same in others? By reframing the words and actions of people I interact with and by adopting a new understanding of their perfection, I am better able to perceive the purity of intention—both theirs and mine.

So, let's review; in order to surrender and let go of the illusion of separateness, you need compassion and patience. Letting go of the illusion of separateness allows you to reframe the way other people act, and accurately perceive their intentions as well as your own. To even begin to realize that we are all One and there is no separation, you have to get familiar with your discomforts in life and recognize that if you are uncomfortable, it is because someone or something in your life is acting as a mirror, reflecting back to you that which is unwanted!

For instance, through my exchanges with others, I realized that I no longer wanted to experience misunderstandings or anything less than love. I recognized a need to practice releasing my attachment to things and people, until I felt peaceful, whether the object or person was there or not. One of the great benefits of reaching this state of peacefulness is that I no longer feel so disappointed or sad when the object or person is gone. As Arnold Patent says in his book *You Can Have It All*, when I accept that I am part of the natural flow of abundance which is the organic nature of

SPEAK KINDLY TO YOUR SHADOW

Infinite Intelligence, I'll know that no matter what I give up or lose, there is an infinite supply of energy (love) available to replace it.

With my access to this infinite love, I gain clarity in what I *do* want; I choose to offer words of support, compassion and courage to anyone engaging in the excavation of their internal landscape, determined to unearth expressions of happiness, joy, sadness and grief, seeking the light of day. My canvas is paper! And words are the implements at my disposal. As the great Roman poet Ovid once said, *scribere jussit amor—love bade me write.*

So, look around in your life; what mirrors are there? What is being reflected back to you? Is it wanted or unwanted? How does this change your intentions going forward? What choices will you make now? Remember: empowerment is a muscle that we can flex if we choose to!

SANDRA ANNE DAVIS

MAKING THE NOT PERSONAL, PERSONAL

When I first made it known to my friends, family and clients that I was writing this book about the tool of Reframing, my sister's friend, Marsha Jones, who is a retired teacher and Union representative, shared her understanding of reframing with me:

"When difficult situations are viewed from a perspective that is <u>not personal,</u> we are better able to develop understanding and create strategies that maintain the dignity of everyone involved."
—*Marsha Jones*

As I read this perspective, I thought yes; Marsha has provided an example of the traditional mindset of *not* taking things personally, which is exactly the mindset that governed the actions I took in my capacity as a

SPEAK KINDLY TO YOUR SHADOW

Union representative, often parroting this mantra—*not to take things personally*—throughout many negotiations. This mindset teaches us that if we simply don't take things personally, then more problems can be solved! It's a very textbook statement that many of us are familiar with.

However, Marsha's reminder of this mindset has alerted me to the realization that my previous understanding of not taking things personally was actually based on a misconception! I am most grateful to Marsha for this reminder, and will now take the opportunity to *reframe* this perception for you and provide an explanation.

During my work life, I applied this perception of *not* taking things personally without realizing that this perception is solidly rooted in a false understanding, a false belief of me *and* others—me versus others. However, living the Medicine Wheel in conscious awareness all these years has instilled a new understanding of that old belief; there is no me *and* them…that would imply we are all separate and alone. So, in fact, *everything* is personal! How can it be otherwise?

Truly, we are *all one.* Neale Donald Walsh taught us that the only difference between *all one* and *alone* is just one letter L—which stands for Love. When we don't have love, we feel alone. But when we open ourselves to love, we dissipate the illusion of separation. The remembering of being <u>*all one*</u> returns and the situation becomes a comfortable and welcoming experience.

Recognizing that we are not alone, but rather *all one*, and that the only conversation really taking place is with one's self, enables us to recognize attachment to our thoughts, words, and actions. Most significantly, our motivation behind "like" and "don't like". This encourages us to take independent ownership of how we, the 'I', feels. Thus, everything becomes personal and we recognize that even though we may have conflict with others or witness conflict in the world, the way we react or respond is completely on *us*. Instead of saying "You did this" or "You made me feel" we can say "It is my belief that" or "I feel like this when". Because *everything is personal*!

Following is a wonderful example of this: "One day there was a seagull out in the yard at San Quentin Prison. It had been raining and the seagull was there paddling around in a puddle. One of the inmates picked up something in the yard and was about to throw it at the bird. Another inmate, Jarvis, didn't even think twice before he automatically put out his hand to stop the man. Everyone started circling around waiting for a fight. The other inmate was screaming at Jarvis, 'Why'd you do that?' And out of Jarvis's mouth came the words, 'I did that because that bird's got my wings.' Everyone understood! Their minds stopped, their hearts softened, and there was silence. Then they all started laughing and joking with him." This story comes from Pema Chödrön's book *Practicing Peace in Times of War* (2007, pg 33-35).

In this exchange, each man bore witness to the understanding that there is no separation. There are many stories to convey a similar message. In the words of Pema Chödrön: "We must take responsibility when our own heart and mind harden and close. We have to be brave enough to soften what is rigid, to find the soft spot and stay with it. We have to have that kind of courage and exercise patience" (2007, pg 36).

Refraining from taking action involves *patience*, not practice. When we feel aggression in any of its forms—resentment, discrimination, jealousy, complaining, and so forth—it's hard to know what to do. We can apply all the good advice we've heard and have given to other people, but often that doesn't seem to help us (2007, pg 38). Reactivity is an addiction, and like all addictions, it controls our decisions because we have attached a belief to certain situations, whether it's "That person hates me" or "I'm not good enough", and we *react* accordingly to that belief. But remember—responsibility is the ability to respond. If we took responsibility for ourselves in a situation, we would be able to respond! And not simply react.

But how do we begin to cease our addiction to reacting? Relaxing before giving in to the underlying urge to act is paramount. Relaxing allows space and time for reframing. Through experience, I have come to agree with the words of Pema Chödrön that "patience is an antidote to aggression because it dissolves the mean-heartedness that results in us harming one another". Pema also explains that we must resolve to *interrupt the momentum* of this for the rest of our lives with *no attachment to resolution.*

A good example of this is a conversation that my sister Jeanette recently had with her friend. During their discussion, my sister shared her belief that meditation is the only way to quiet the mind. Her friend's response was a question: "But what about all the time you spend reading?" My sister replied, "Well for me, reading is a form of escape, a guilty pleasure! Certainly not something I would equate with meditation."

Her friend's response was, "Interesting. The form of distraction you choose is one that allows you to distance yourself from all the chatter around you and inside your head. Thereby providing you exactly what other forms of meditation offer for others!" This reply sums up Pema's explanation perfectly. My sister's friend interrupted the momentum of a belief my sister had about meditation while having *no attachment to resolution.* Now, my sister views her reading habits as a form of much-needed meditation rather than a guilty pleasure!

SPEAK KINDLY TO YOUR SHADOW

So, let's review: by interrupting the momentum of beliefs, reactivity and aggression through relaxing and being patient, we allow space for reframing, which leads to the formation of new, more accurate beliefs about a situation. During this pause and reflection, we can begin to take responsibility for our part in something, even if it's a situation about someone else or a conflict in the world that seems very far away. We have a responsibility to it because everything is personal, because we are all one, all connected. If we continue to believe in the illusion that we are all separate from each other, animals, earth and even our own selves, and we take nothing personally except that which wounds our ego, we will continue to feed an addiction to reactivity and passivity. We may choose to not help someone, because we believe it has nothing to do with us when in fact it does!

The best way I can think to explain this succinctly is to say—if you saw someone in trouble, or someone suffering or being treated unjustly, you wouldn't want that done to you, would you? Therefore, it *is* personal. Everything is, because we're *all one.*

THE POWER OF WORDS: REFRAMING CONCEPTS WITH ACRONYMS

During further discussion with my sister regarding Reframing and its necessity, she requested that I provide some examples of specific words and how I might reframe them. She gave the example of the word "suffering" and explained that the concept of suffering is a challenge for her, and many of her friends and family. Since I've commonly used acronyms as a form of expression throughout my spiritual journey, I will now take the time in this chapter to provide examples of how I use acronyms to provide new interpretations of common words, for the express purpose of Reframing. I must credit my Medicine Man Woody for this, and express my deep gratitude to him for igniting my understanding of situations through the use of acronyms.

Everyone finds the understanding of suffering to be challenging, not merely as a concept, but also in understanding how suffering could possibly serve us on our journey! The traditional definition of suffering or to suffer is "to experience or be subjected to something bad or unpleasant." However, using the power of acronyms, I reframe the word 'suffer' as: **S**anctioning **U**lterior **F**alsehood **F**or **E**rroneous **R**etribution.

Essentially, this reframes suffering as: allowing ourselves to be subject to a false belief in punishment. Because if you think about it—why *do* we suffer? Why do we accept suffering as a natural condition in our lives and the lives of others when it causes such distress? Is the pain and discomfort created through the act of suffering erroneous? Is the need for it false? And if so, why do we sanction it? Could it be that we have ulterior motives? If suffering is just another choice, another life experience, then it is not difficult to understand how suffering serves us on our journey, thereby making it a necessary part of our current human conditioning.

I know the idea of *choosing* to suffer may seem counterintuitive and improbable; after all who would *willingly* choose to suffer?

And yet, when we feel like we're suffering, it's because we *are* choosing it. We allow ourselves to suffer perhaps because we have a victim mindset and are attached to a belief that nothing is ever our fault. Or perhaps because we unconsciously desire to punish ourselves for some unresolved reason. Or maybe we choose to suffer because we don't know who we are if we allow peace and happiness into our life. In other words, our identity is wrapped up in suffering—who would I be if I didn't have anything to complain about?

Indeed, suffering is a challenging concept to grasp and take ownership of, because no one wants to believe that they willingly choose misery! But many people do all the time. However, I want to emphasize that it's *okay* to choose suffering, because ultimately the lessons we learn around it will serve us on our journey.

Other examples that relate directly to suffering:

FEAR:

False Expectations Appearing Real or
False Evidence Appearing Real

HATE:

Having Anger Threatening Existence

PAIN:

Putting Anger In Neutral

If we fear something, we have a false expectation of something being real when it isn't, and we may feel threatened or become angered, thereby awakening our fight or flight response to this imagined wrongdoing or enemy (the thing we now fear). Anger can lead to hate, where our existence now feels threatened. Self-preservation kicks in! We make choices based on survival, we attempt to put our anger into neutral, which only creates more pain, thus we suffer—all under the guise of erroneous retribution!

Words are a great reframing tool because words are simply that—words. Any word is open to new interpretation through the use of acronyms, even the word love: **l**etting **o**ur **v**alues **e**merge. Much of language only serves to provide a way to understand what we are witnessing, but it is powerful because the terminology we use determines our worldview. Thus, reframing words through acronyms can quite literally alter our reality!

The word 'suffer' is such a great example of how our worldview can change, depending on how we understand the meaning of suffering. With suffering, most times it is religious dogma that feeds the mind with the falsehood that suffering is ordained by God and that the more a person suffers on earth, the greater the rewards in heaven. Essentially, the idea of washing away sin is a man-made concept, and 'suffering' has been wrapped up in that false belief over many centuries. Thus, our indoctrination as a society has fed us a falsehood that suffering is ordained by God! But this is not true; however, it explains our willingness to accept suffering and to even encourage it. To heal this false belief around the word 'suffering' and any other words whose meaning we derive from ancient religious texts, we must first reframe what we believe about God, beginning with a new understanding that we are *not* separate from God. Any belief of separation is an illusion!

So, who or what is God? God is love (energy) and love is God expressed. Expression is demonstration. Therefore, we come face to face with God in all our exchanges when we *govern ourselves divinely*. God asks nothing of us; it is we who determine how we will respond to the presence of God (love) in every situation. How could a God like that possibly ordain suffering? It's clear; the manifestation of our choice is staring us in the face, a choice to accept responsibility to govern oneself with power and authority by expressing our individual reflection of the divine through self-love and acceptance. Suffering, then, is a very clear example of our collective choice, only one of many, to *not* govern ourselves divinely.

Mirror mirror on the wall
Who is the fairest of them all?
You of course! Could there be any doubt?
Your smile lights up the sun, to bring light into the world
Your tears bring the rain, to cleanse and refresh

SPEAK KINDLY TO YOUR SHADOW

Your happiness creates rainbows, that dance on distant hillsides
Your sadness excavates the unstable, and provides clarity
You are the 'wonder' of this world and beyond....
  —Sandra Anne Davis

HAVING FAITH

The benefits from writing this book as a memoir became clearer the more I wrote, for the way in which I have been guided has ultimately been a journey of reframing! Unearthing the recognition of the little girl, the orphan within, was of the gravest significance. Through her view of the world, I realized that my present-day perceptions were being formed, hard and fast. Why was this?

As a little girl, my experience of trust, or rather, lack thereof, disallowed intimacy. By fearing for my safety at every turn, unable to trust anything, I was blinded to alternative perceptions that could have allowed for more peace and love, thus I remained locked in a prison of my own design. As my insight developed, I rallied against this prison, ultimately coming to an understanding that was gifted to me by an unknown voice, my inner voice. This voice distinguished God's vocabulary from the external chatter of other people that at times threatened my very existence. The understanding this inner voice gave to me was that trust was mandatory! There could be no hope of authenticity without it.

Recognizing that a quiet and fearless voice is constantly available to me has to be practiced. Without it, I live on autopilot! I react instead of responding. I put up barriers and create a sense of "me" as separate from "you". Clearly, this little girl was my nemesis, or at least my antagonist! But when I acknowledge her defiance, I can better understand—because recognition and acceptance always precede inner-knowing (*Sacred Path Cards*, Jamie Sams, pg. 61).

How exactly did I do this? By trusting. Once I recognized it, whatever *it* was, I then needed to accept it. Faith proved to be the necessary component, and it seemed that having faith was as natural for me as breathing. Faith, by its very nature, required me to remain detached so that I didn't erect barriers, because you cannot have faith if you're attached to outcomes. It allowed me to be present without denying what I was feeling, staying open to the difficulties and becoming intimate with the pain, the discomfort. Only by allowing the feelings could I recognize the discrepancies.

Inviting awareness revealed contradictory beliefs I was beholden to, as evidenced in my many marriages: not good enough, not smart enough, not soft enough, not vulnerable enough, not male enough, not worthy enough, not valuable enough. Put plain and simple—not enough! Clearly, believing I was not enough coloured the relationships I entered into. These relationships, these men, didn't stand a chance at making the relationship work!

What did I do with this fixed perception of myself as *not enough*? I cloaked it! Avoided it. Disguised it. Because of this, no matter what contribution either myself or my partners made, the perfectionism we sought in our relationships could never be found. Marriage offers a platform, a stage upon which we act out and experience firsthand knowledge of our human frailties. We create and engage another soul in portraying roles of comparison! And best of all, this stage is an effective barometer of self-love. As you can imagine, my barometer of self-love was pretty low due to my beliefs of not being enough. But when I exercised faith—faith in myself, faith in the situation, faith in others, faith in God—everything became possible.

SPEAK KINDLY TO YOUR SHADOW

HOW NOT TO RUN AWAY

On my journey to faith, and finding acceptance through help, hope, and humanity, I was blessed to receive a key from Angel Doll Barulious. I will now share with you a summarized version of the story of Angel Doll Barulious taken from my book *Angels Do the Darndest Things!*

Barulious was an angel doll crafted for me by my friend Elsie Poliquin. She wanted me to provide her with Inner Child therapy sessions and in exchange, she wished to provide this angel doll. He is the physical representation of an angel, dressed in the finest damask robe, topped by a vibrant blue silk cloak. I was in awe at the size and detail of his wings and was intrigued by the ornate key suspended from a gold chain around his neck. In his right hand, he carried a long staff adorned with a magnificent quartz crystal in the shape of a hexagon. Quartz is said to be a very spiritual stone, harmonizing the energies of the universe with the human energies of thoughts, consciousness and emotions (*Crystal Deva Cards*, Cindy Watlington).

The key Barulious wore around his neck reminded me of a dream I experienced. In the dream, I'm wearing a dress with pockets. Intuitively, I reach into a pocket with my left hand and find an old, tarnished metal key. I roll the key around in my palm, noting its size and weight. After returning the key to my pocket, I follow an internal compass to a massive cedar tree with an uncommonly large hole. A comforting voice tells me to reach in and pull out what I find. Inside is another key, which I lift out with both hands. It's a very large wooden key, ornately carved. However, despite its large size, it is exceptionally light; not what I anticipated at all! The meaning of the two keys in my dream pointed to an understanding that all was not as it seemed on the surface because perception—personal bias—is always looming.

The memory of this dream was brought forth by the significance of the key that Angel Doll Barulious wears. Thanks to him, I realized that it's necessary for me to accept the gift of my keys in whatever form they are presented. The key he brought me was the key to unlocking our ability to receive and nurture our inner child. This can only happen when safety and trust are established.

If the child harbours fear of any kind, they lose their ability to be vulnerable, thereby developing a prison of their own making! And so, Barulious became a source of comfort and support as I navigated new paths, overcoming challenges with love and guidance. He taught me that becoming intimate with pain and staying open to everything I experience is the key to transforming at the core of my being. By letting the sharpness of difficult times pierce me to the heart, it would open me, humble me, and make me wiser and braver…and so it did.

It would seem that Barulious had come to teach me what Pema Chödrön alluded to when she wrote about the need for *"how not to run away."* Through the help and guidance of angel Barulious, I was finally able to distinguish between the illusion of being a victim in fear (false expectations appearing real) and the desire to escape! As well as the truth that no separation exists. How can I run? Where can I go when all paths lead back to me?

My defiant stance as that little girl, "I may have to be here but I don't have to like it!" was an interesting one. Often when I heard myself iterate this belief, I recognized an intense defiance and truth be told, I relished it! It felt like I was saying, "Do whatever you want to me. Do your worst, but know that I am the boss. I'm the one in charge!" I remember with some clarity an incident of defiance with my stepfather. He had discovered that my younger sister had allowed her friend to join us in our back yard to play under the sprinkler, after leaving strict instructions to the contrary. My sister and I were to remain home alone until he returned. So, when he did come home and realized that we had disobeyed him, he was irate.

Apparently, what gave us away were the three wet towels drying on the clothesline. The first thing our stepfather did was make my sister and I stand in front of him. For us, it felt like we were facing a firing squad! With suspicious intent, he demanded to know if we had a friend over while he was not at home.

"No, I did not," was my reply. And so, too, was my sister's.

"Well, I know you are lying because there are three wet towels on the line," he declared.

Now, I could be mistaken, but I always felt he knew it was my sister Karon's friend Judy. Why I believed this I can't really say. However, after his threat of only one more chance to tell the truth, both Karon and I repeated our first response. I must admit I was frustrated that my sister wouldn't just tell him the truth about her friend being there. But knowing her fear of his abuse, I could certainly understand her silence.

I, on the other hand, was telling the truth; I did not have a friend over against his wishes, and therefore it was not my friend's towel on the line. But Alex being Alex, he chose me as that day's target. There never seemed to be rhyme nor reason in his decisions…

"So Sandy, I will ask you again; did you have a friend over?"

"No, I did not." Whack! A hard slap across my face.

"Now Sandy, I will ask you again."

"And again, I will give you the same answer. No, I did not!" Whack! Another slap across my face, only this time on the other side. I remember thinking about the bible passage *"turn the other cheek"*.

SPEAK KINDLY TO YOUR SHADOW

Again, the question, and again the same answer, my defiance growing stronger with each slap. First one side then the other, his anger and frustration increasing with each additional blow! I could barely hear my sister screaming and crying with the ringing in my ears.

Then suddenly, it stopped. My sister Karon and I were sent upstairs to our room. She tried desperately to comfort me, but all I seemed able to do was stare at her. I was in pain and couldn't hear anything but the ringing. Yet, I had not cried. I was still in charge; I was content.

This is only one of many acts of defiance that span a lifetime. *"I may have to be here, but I don't have to like it"* was my mantra, an affirmation of my willingness to defy and protect my right to decide, my right to choose—decide and choose *what* exactly, I'm not sure. Could this defiance be one and the same with this idea of 'not running away' that Pema Chödrön alludes to? After all, it appears that my defiance allowed me to circumvent any reality where I was being victimized, and instead, stand my ground with a warrior heart. But this *also* allowed me to stay fully invested in the illusion of separation—me versus them—an illusion that cloaked the truth that whenever my stepfather Alex slapped me, he was actually abusing himself too, just like Jarvis and the bird in the prison yard.

Perhaps my defiance was the most effective tool at my disposal, making it a healthier choice than I realize…maybe yes, maybe no. Remembering that I am a decider and that choice is *my* birthright is most certainly worth protecting. Even more significant is my inner child's recognition of a voice, a clear and reliable communicator who has never been acclimated or bastardised. A pure voice that could be trusted. A voice I have come to recognize and accept.

This recognition frees me to see the entirety of my lifetime from a new perspective. There are no bad or wrong choices; defiance was my tool, and evidently, Alex and my sister required the mirror of defiance for their personal experience. I was their gift and they were mine! We all bore witness to *choice*! Life is the reflection of what we believe, plain and simple, and my willingness to offer the mirror of defiance provided them with a look at what was unconscious in them—what *they* had cloaked in an effort not to see!

My choice of defiance provided me with a sense of power. However, the acts of defiance kept me separate from my feelings, from the true barometer of love. In my naivety, I actually believed that I was not running away from anything; I was just standing my ground! Choosing was always at the forefront of my decision making, whatever the decisions were.

In summation, the following methods assisted me in reframing:

1. Using mirroring as a gift for bearing witness to myself and others in all situations
2. Recognizing that we are not alone but rather <u>all one</u>, which makes everything personal and eliminates the need to default to blame and shame.
3. Seeing words through the lens of acronyms to better understand the deeper meaning behind culturally-tainted concepts like 'suffering' and 'pain'
4. Choosing to have faith in situations and trusting the process; be it one of pain, joy, sadness, laughter or suffering!
5. Becoming intimate with the aforementioned situations and moving through them rather than running away.

Robert Frost is credited with saying "the only way out is through." My introduction to this concept came from Carl Jung. What really matters here is the strength of this message. It is a significant revelation about our earthly sojourn and the need for experience. Who would I be if I hadn't been defiant? What would have happened? While I cannot answer these questions, I have come to believe that there are no accidents or missed opportunities; not all opportunities are for us. Everything happens for a reason, and this book is reason enough for why I chose the journey that served me. I found the way through, ultimately allowing me to share insights and newly developed perceptions with you.

Through this methodology I learned that what I perceived as defiance was my way of running! Running away from the pain and suffering of that which was truly out of my control. And the light bulb moment was realizing that my determination to run was counterproductive. All I accomplished was to internalize my feelings, burying them so deep that without my personal commitment to excavation, I may well have imploded!

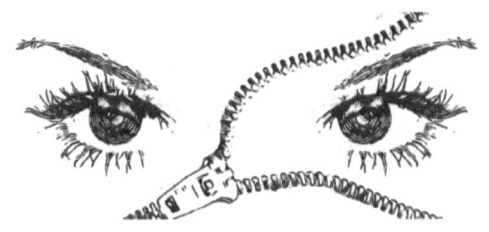

CHAPTER FIVE: DEATH, THE UNPLANNED CHAPTER

A LOVE STORY COMPLETED

This chapter was entirely unplanned, just as death and dying so often are. During March of 2024, I had just reached the end of writing this manuscript. Before the final revision by my editor began, my husband of 11 years, my friend of 38 years and my soulmate, Rick, became ill quite suddenly. He was diagnosed with advanced stage four Pancreatic Cancer!

Our time together during those last weeks was precious to us both.

At my husband's request, he stayed with me in our log home. While he was still able to, we walked our acreage and sat by the brook. We talked and laughed and reminisced and we realized in those moments, the gift we had been given in our move to New Brunswick. We came to the realization that coming together later in life was our way of completing the final chapter of our book, our story. We had come together to experience it all—friendship, love, compassion, sensuality, joy, sexuality, laughter, and fun! *Hell yes!* We finally understood that our long-term friendship provided the solid foundation that carried us to this place together. Our last eleven years were just the long-awaited culmination of our souls' journey together.

It did not take long for my new role as his nurse to kick in. As the front-line personal care provider for a loved one, the most important thing becomes their medical treatment. This requires the discipline to follow detailed instructions provided by the doctors and nurses involved in managing the illness. Monitoring and executing every detail of the patient's well-being often takes precedence over their desire to be left alone.

Although I was a parent with children who often required medical care and attention, this did not prepare me in *any* way for the challenges of meeting the needs of my husband! He was, after all, an adult. He had been making choices and decisions for himself his entire life. Neither he nor I wanted this to change. We were comfortable in our agreed upon roles in marriage and our independent relationships. We had worked towards an honourable and respectful means of interacting with each other for the duration of our 38+ year relationship. During my husband's illness, there was a definite shift and a resistance by both of us to accept these new changes that were so foreign.

But time together was the most precious thing we had left to share, and so we both soldiered on with this new arrangement of nurse-patient. The demands and schedules for all his medications, injections, and IVs was challenging for me while he was at home. Although I was honoured to provide him with this kind of care, I also came to recognize the loss of just being his loving wife and instead becoming his nurse! It was challenging for both of us, but I was truly blessed to be his caregiver in every way up until the last four days of his life when he was moved to hospice.

It was Dr. MacDonald who convinced me to move Rick to Hospice Fredericton. Here, he suggested, we would be able to spend those final days together as husband and wife, while Rick's palliative team took care of him. Expressing my thanks to Dr. MacDonald for being so insightful, and the generous, wonderful care provided by Hospice Fredericton, will be a lifetime endeavour. Laying by Rick's side in his hospital bed was salve for my aching heart! The incredible staff at Hospice Fredericton were so much more capable than I in keeping Rick comfortable. Finally, we were able to have those last precious days together just as husband and wife, as the souls we are, here to walk each other home.

~

I am now convinced that both my husband and I had a misunderstanding of the true benefits of hospice care prior to going there. We, like so many others, perceived hospice as the final acceptance of the imminence of death—end of story! We thought that deciding to go to hospice meant you were giving up on your loved one or enabling them to give up on themselves. That by choosing the amazing care and comfort being offered by hospice, you must be, on some level, accepting a death sentence! But these were all *false beliefs*!

"You matter because you are you. You matter until the last moment of your life, and we will do all we can to help you not only to die peacefully, but also to live until you die."
–Dame Cicely Saunders

This quote is by one of the most influential female figures of the 20th century, Dame Cicely Saunders. She was responsible for transforming the way society viewed care for the dying. Cicely was the founder of the modern hospice movement and her legacy continues to affect how many of us will be cared for as we approach the end of our lives. Her new ideas of person-centred care emerged from her unique multi-disciplined experience as a nurse, medical social worker, doctor and researcher. She introduced effective pain management and the concept of "total pain", the idea that suffering encompasses all of a person's physical, psychological, social, spiritual, and practical struggles.

After observing hospice implementing 'total pain' management for my husband's comfort and previously having such false beliefs about what hospice really means, it now appears to me that society has successfully placed an unwarranted sense of responsibility and fear on families! This has created insurmountable challenges for all parties involved in end-of-life decisions! Society, as a whole, feels alienated when it comes to matters of death, which makes us fearful when taking action and making choices on behalf of our loved ones facing this situation.

What if we make the 'wrong' decision? What if we regret something later on? What if our actions inadvertently make the situation worse for our loved one? In this sense, we might consider the cost to *all* who are involved in someone's end-of-life. I'm talking about more than just medical costs; I'm concerned about what Dame Cicely Saunders refers to as "total pain". Essentially, the physical, psychological, social, spiritual, and practical struggles and wellbeing of not just the loved one facing death, but of all the family members directly involved in the person's end-of-life management. They too are being seriously affected by any and all decisions being made.

But making the decision to choose hospice as an alternative end-of-life care for our loved one, is a valuable consideration! It's a decision that I personally have come to recognize as a wise and healthy choice. Comfort, respect, attention, and commitment to the wishes of the hospice resident and their families is crucial during such a transformational time. It is not possible for me to express the *gratitude* that Rick and I share for Dr. MacDonald and the hospice palliative team, as well as Extramural Fredericton, and all the Horizon Medical staff of doctors and nurses. Their medical expertise during Rick's health care process with unmitigated **Compassion** and **Grace**, navigated us with a calm surety through Rick's end-of-life journey.

DEATH AND LIFE GO TOGETHER

On Saturday, May 18th, 2024, at 7:20 am, I was honoured to be lying beside my husband Rick as he took his final breath. I was there as we agreed, to be with him for that final walk.

I am including this additional chapter in *Speak Kindly To Your Shadow* at the request of the wonderful nurses from Extramural Fredericton that assisted me with Rick's at-home care. They shared with me a common perception in their line of work, which is that the ultimate reframe for life is in fact death.

Death and dying is the essence of our being here. We actually live this process on a daily basis, from the time we are born and inhale our first breath, until the moment we exhale our last breath. I was there to bear witness to my husband's life, and I was there as the last breath left his body. Lying in bed next to him, I observed the quietest, most gentle breath I've ever witnessed, and the complete relaxation of his entire body. His eyes were closed and his face was soft and gentle like his beautiful heart.

Living and dying go hand in hand. They are made up of the same polarities as the earth's axis! On this planet, it is not possible to experience one without the other. Being born in the earth's energy is an experience of awe and wonder. It is also the first experience of separation! When a child leaves the safety of the mother's womb, there is a sense of disconnect. The trip through the birth canal, or being lifted from the mother's womb directly, leaves the newborn child in a state of separation. What was, isn't anymore!

SPEAK KINDLY TO YOUR SHADOW

Then begins the search to feel whole again. This desire to *reconnect* shapes our journey, and from this perception of the world, the human experience is filtered through a belief in separation, a sense of not belonging, of not fitting in, of feeling somehow incomplete. And so begins the illusion of separation from God, and humanity's own trail of tears.

After experiencing Rick's death, I do see the reframe the nurses are alluding to; loss of this magnitude felt unbearable! My heart hurt so badly that I worried for it. I was unsure of its ability to hold up, to stay strong and not crumble and collapse. In this state of flux, I was concerned for a future, any future, that did not have my husband in it—could there be anything after us? How? I dared to ask these questions during such a time of grief.

SANDRA ANNE DAVIS

CHOICE LIVES ON

Then I remembered, and allowed myself to go through all those feelings. I willed myself to be in the pain of loss and grief, to feel the intensity of the emotions seeping from the walls of our log home! Infiltrating not only my days but also the fragments of sleep that were fleeting. How was it possible? How could our house, our home, remain alive through ruin, wreckage and irreparable annihilation? Does it not know? Can it be so oblivious, so unaware that without the foundation it will crumble and collapse? Can it be so unfair as to think it will go on? Does it not know that I need it to give way! That my heart begs for relief...my husband made me a promise! We would be together until there was no breath left in my body. He would not leave me; he would always be here by my side. It was *he* who would comfort me until my last breath. That was our agreement. I would cease to wander and he would hold a welcome space for me. A space of love, kindness, joy and above all else laughter!

Yet here I am, alone and still in choice.

As I continue to allow all of it, the gifts that our relationship provided will sustain me going forward in life. Not just me, but others—those who knew my husband and those who were not blessed to. Because life is movement and so is death. The energies are the same, only the vibration is different. My husband had a journey significant for his expression in the world, as do all of us. My gift to him is in maintaining an understanding of this. As partners, we made agreements of the heart that surpass all understanding. He and I chose each other for the mirrors we each provided, the reflections we gave to each other. I got him and he got me! There is no greater acquisition in life than to acquire an authentic reflection of love.

This is a gratitude worth embracing. I *choose* to embrace it because life goes on.

Reframing becomes most beneficial here by shifting the concept of death to life. In this way, I'm able to see the continuation of life, the cyclical laws of nature in action. Since we are not alone and are *all one*, and energy can neither be created nor destroyed, only transmuted, I know that my husband has not left me. There is no separation. Any other perception is therefore an illusion, an investment in fear—false expectations appearing real. And I have come to discover that the greatest falsehood—our collective fear—is the lie, the illusion, that we are separate from each other and ultimately from God!

What I know in my heart is what I know of God and governing oneself divinely: the reality of separation's illusory nature is confirmed through the experience of death and dying, and this is a truth I must be wholly present and aligned with. Yes, the physical and emotional pain of loss is tangible and at times debilitating, further feeding the belief in an apparent separation, yet it is part of life, which truly defines our connection to each other and to everything else.

I can personally attest to this. As of late, signs from the universe have provided affirmations of my progress during my grieving process. I woke up one morning at 3:33am. This happens frequently, always during the night; 4:44 am, 3:33 am, and often at 11:11 pm. These are angel numbers, signals of the appropriateness of the journey my husband Rick and I are still sharing. In life there is death, and in death, there is still life.

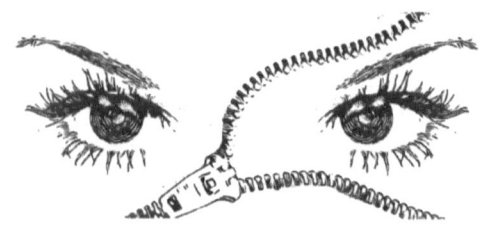

CHAPTER SIX: AN INVITATION TO REFRAME

YOU, TOO, CAN REFRAME

It is my hope that you can now see that reframing is available to you and to us all! The very air you breathe will become more familiar and much friendlier once you are willing to *speak kindly to your shadow.* The world is not friendly, nor is nature; but that is not their purpose. Because they're organic, they function authentically. We, on the other hand, have lost sight of the truth: *there is no separation!* We, like nature herself, are organic—waves in the ocean of God designed in perfect rhythm with the beating of our collective heart! Moving in…and out. Constant, but not consistent. Perfect within a landscape of perceived imperfection.

You may be in a position where you feel you need support and guidance, and you feel lost and don't know how to move forward. I can safely say I've been in the same place, but I am now able to reframe situations I find myself in. Because of this, I can say with surety that you can do it too! You can make a new decision to traverse obstacles that you have participated in creating, because everything is a choice. You, too, can set out to pave a new road with a new designation in mind. Often it is the road less travelled, but that is the beauty of governing oneself divinely—we begin to make intentional choices!

Consider this your formal invitation to begin reframing your life and the narratives in it that have held you back. The mind does not see reality; it *creates* reality. You, too, can create your reality through the tool of reframing.

If you are feeling at a loss with this shift in perspective, do not fear, for there are numerous tools at your disposal to help guide you. Let me explain.

CONSULTING WITH YOURSELF

Through my experience with the Bible, various insightful books, Medicine Cards, Sacred Pathway Cards, Angel Blessing Cards, Runes and other oracles, I have found many of them to be welcome tools and instrumental in guiding me deeper and deeper into the depths—the core—of not just me, but of everything, guiding me to that place of compassion and grace. I have embraced many forms of research and documentation throughout my earthly sojourn. But always, and consistently, the words of wisdom I receive as part of my daily meditation provides guidance when I need it most. There have been many forms of communication with the Divine throughout my lifetime in these meditations, and through other means. For instance, I have sought guidance and comfort through the Bible from the words of those who came before. The messages I receive always address what it is I am currently dealing with and serve to remind me of my responsibility, the ability to respond in any situation.

When I meditate or consult the Bible, books of insight, or any kind of oracle card, what I'm really doing is *consulting with myself.* I'm reminded of a quote from Ralph H Blum's *The Book of Runes:*

Lift up the self by the Self
And don't let the self droop down,
For the Self is the self's only friend
And the self is the Self's only foe.

During these self-consultations, movement is assured through my willingness to allow the words to resonate within the core of my being. And often, the guidance I receive is to *be still*. Self-change is never coerced. There's a time to excavate, and a time to be still. In the words of St. Augustine, "The reward of patience is patience." Essentially, do without doing, and everything gets done! But we must also remember, "More than we are doers, we are deciders" (*The Book of Ruins*, Ralph H. Blum, pg 109). Decision begets action, and sometimes that action is to simply *be still.* This is the wisdom I have received from consulting with myself through various divining tools for insight.

However, unfortunately throughout history, the use of oracle cards and other divination tools has been defamed, and thus, through the determination of critics, the benefits of these amazing tools are being disparaged! But this could not be further from

SPEAK KINDLY TO YOUR SHADOW

the truth, and I would like to offer a neutral and unbiased *reframe*.

If we choose to see divination tools, like oracle cards, Tarot[xviii], Medicine Cards, and Runes, in a way that is akin to that of the Bible, the Book of Certitude, and even the Torah, then they become invaluable commodities! If you pick up the Bible or any similar type of book, or any divination tool such as runes or tarot, you will *always* find the answer, because you are accessing the answer from within you. "Ask and you shall receive" as Jesus said. Seek and you shall find. The vehicle you use for seeking does not matter. The fact you are asking at all guarantees the answer you're looking for, even if you're not conscious of it yet. **The key is to trust!** Trust is tied to our belief system—not the tools we use for guidance. If you're asking questions from a place (a belief system) that you trust, then with the help of our Shadow, *our authenticity will not mislead us*. It is not even possible! Because everything divine is natural, beautiful and eternal. True beauty is always new, never going out of style. When consulting with yourself, you are attuned with your *Eternal Self*, and you express the harmony that is your unique reflection of God (*Angel Blessings: Cards of Sacred Guidance and Inspiration*, Kimberly Marooney).

Through these forms of divination, we benefit from support and guidance that has been provided to us since immemorial time. By embracing this knowledge, ancient or modern, we are assisted in awakening to core beliefs—and herein lies the true value! With this newfound collaboration, we are assisted in accessing the dark and hidden places within us that harbour <u>self-loathing</u> and <u>intolerance</u>, places that we wouldn't normally see otherwise because we've cloaked them. But everyone is capable of shedding this secrecy. To find something that appears lost (that which we have no conscious memory of) requires light! As I have said before, the Shadow offers us reflection, thereby allowing us to look at and befriend whatever *it is* that we have kept at bay in the dark. With these forms of guidance, tools of divination, reframing, we are guided forward with a new light of understanding.

As such, it should come as no surprise that I am currently creating a deck of cards to accompany *Speak Kindly To Your Shadow*. I am pleased to create these cards as a handy tool for understanding daily situations that arise in your life, situations that require you to reframe your perception in that moment. These cards can be used whenever you feel the need for the divine guidance that resides within you.

So as requested by clients, friends and family alike, a deck of cards with a small guidebook will be made available in the near future. Whether you decide that this book alone, *Speak Kindly To Your Shadow,* is sufficient for your purposes, or you decide to purchase the soon-to-be-available companion cards, I'm confident in your ability to incorporate reframing successfully in your daily life. Choice is your personal power. Embrace it!

THE SHADOW SPEAKS

I would like to take this time to review and summarize all that has been shared up to this point, all that the Shadow has provided. One of the biggest takeaways that I hope you've caught on to is that the power of the Shadow has always been about *reflection*. What we see in others is, and always has been, a reflection of us! This is what makes everything personal. There is a great passage by Arnold Patent that expands further the importance of reflection and mirrors:

"Reflection is all about mirrors! Everything that we see and feel is a reflection of the state of our own consciousness. In more concrete terms, every

SPEAK KINDLY TO YOUR SHADOW

person that we see is showing us some aspect of who we are. Everything that we come into contact with reflects to us something about ourselves we might not know. Every feeling that is felt or expressed by another, mirrors a feeling deep within each of us. Our human experience is like a hall of mirrors and is a gift of the highest order. There is no greater learning method than demonstration, and the more we learn about ourselves, the greater value our lives have. Seeing ourselves surrounded by mirrors at all times, we realize that whatever is going on is just our state of consciousness being reflected back to us. And our state of consciousness is an accurate reflection of how much love we feel for ourselves. We are always having an experience with ourselves even though others may be involved. This is a tricky concept to accept. But when we are able to appreciate the concept, our lives will become simpler, and we will find it easier to feel love for ourselves as well as for others."

Arnold is right; it is a tricky concept to accept, let alone appreciate! But remember, it doesn't take practice—it takes *patience*. Patience disrupts the momentum of negative thoughts and feelings; it forces a moment of pause where we can breathe and accurately reflect on what is going on around us. It makes room for compassion.

I am no saint; I struggled with this concept for a long time. Through my defiant determination to stand against anything that reflected less than what I wanted to believe about myself, I remained separate from the truth of me. It was only through my commitment to understanding God—governing oneself divinely—and responsibility—the ability to respond—that I came to know and embrace the importance of individuality within a framework of interdependence. Over time, the developed relationship with my Shadow helped me reframe the old belief system of the little girl inside me, the belief that said definitively, "I may have to be here, but I don't have to like it!" My Shadow reframed this message and now, that little girl's words are salve to my soul: "I am not dirty or hungry or injured. I am as I have always been, whole and complete. I am not healed for I've never been broken. I am what you are...*perfect.*"[xix]

Finally, she has spoken! The Shadow who has been witness to it all. Through her, I hear and know how truly blessed I am and have always been. She has been calling softly, gently, nudging me like the cold wet nose of our companion, the dog—loyal, steadfast and true. And just as importantly, she is reliable. She has allowed me to see that I am a wave in the ocean of God, and as such I am one with the entire ocean, with you! There is no possibility of anything else. Yet, I have been manipulating the reflections by being selective in the ones that I chose to embrace while cloaking others in darkness. My defiance was my salvation but it kept me distanced from the truth.

Through the Shadow, I have been provided with the brilliance of the sun's rays. Just like in the story of The Little Tree, I have come to experience the warmth, the beauty and strength I possess. I am enamoured; I am in love with me, myself and I...*now I understand.* It took many things, many experiences, and many people to get here, but above all it took faith! Having faith so I could trust again. Trust allowed me to move *through* experiences and feel everything that I had unconsciously agreed to, rather than run away and avoid. Many of the choices I made in my early life were *unconscious* choices; I did not know I was making choices based on illusions and false beliefs! But as soon as you see a magic trick, an illusion, for what it is, it disappears. You can then make intentional conscious choices, which is very empowering. My Shadow allowed space for me to consciously choose, and yours can too.

If any of this is feeling overwhelming or abstract, I want to remind you again of the tools of divination at your disposal (oracle cards, runes, I Ching, meditation, and many others) as well as the best place to start—*mirrors*. The power of reflection truly is the foundation to reframing any situation. Just as Jesus wanted us to realize that in our desire to love, we must first begin with the self—the little self; that which is earth-bound and relies on reflections! The son was here on earth to provide the perfect mirror of God, the father, that which he himself was. Jesus knew better than we that there is no separation between himself and God. They are one. In his time on earth, he spent many years studying all over the world, listening to alternative beliefs and perspectives, determining that the best way forward is through the knowledge of eternal life! There was no beginning and no end to God. God is love and love is God expressed in the world! God just *is*.

Through the art of mirroring, Jesus shared his understanding of God's reflection with everyone he came into contact with. The disciples, his tribe, and everyone else. Yes, even his enemies! Mirrors are not good or bad; they simply reflect. As Chinese philosopher Chuang Tzu says, "The perfect man is but a mirror, he leans neither forward nor backward, he remains unchanged." Jesus provided the ultimate mirror of human behaviour and its expansiveness. He held a space of compassion, often without empathy or judgement, and led with grace. He developed no illusions about nature, human or otherwise. He just walked and talked in authenticity. Moving through life authentically with no attachments, and most significantly, with no desire for resolution. This is and always was the simplicity of his message. So, I implore you, if you aren't sure where to start, start with mirrors and recognizing the reflections in your life, and what they show you about yourself.

Now we have come to the natural end. All that needs to be said, has been said. The Shadow has spoken. It is my intention that this book activates a familiar way for you to reframe that place in your life and all your experiences, simply by listening to your Shadow and honouring all your exchanges. As an authentic witness, she will guide you. The willingness to surrender all your preconceived notions and ideas will allow you to create a revised perception of this world that aligns more deeply with your authenticity than any perceptions that came before. Through the act of reframing, the true energy of source—of *love*—will be evident in all its glory!

And now, I must take this moment to end with a big thank you to many of the mirrors I've experienced in my life…

SANDRA ANNE DAVIS

Thank you, Alex. Thank you to my husband Rick. Thank you to all my husbands and each of my wonderful neighbours.

Thank you, friends and enemies, alike. Thank you, siblings and parents and relatives. Doctors and nurses and strangers…A very specific expression of sincere gratitude to Dr. Roberto Hernandez Gonzalez and Alain Johnston from Stanly, Dr. Greg Thompson of Fredericton, Dr. Burnell and Dr. Mohudin Oncology Saint John, New Brunswick.

Thank you to my dearest children and grandchildren and stepchildren and each and every animal and pet I have been blessed to share my life with!

Thank you, with gratitude and thanksgiving to my teachers, the medicine men and women and all the ancestors.

It is through your gift of mirroring that my life has been laid bare. Your willingness to expose all is a testament to your authenticity and your immense courage and bravery.

SPEAK KINDLY TO YOUR SHADOW

Another of my great loves are the horses, and their profound teachings through intimacy!

To my many and wonderful clients, and those of you I have not met and may never in this lifetime, thank you. Thank you, Great Spirit, and all my 'Relations' miigwech, Ho!

The End.

SANDRA ANNE DAVIS

AFTERWORD

As I wrote this book *Speak Kindly To Your Shadow,* a metamorphosis took place. In my desire to fulfill the requests of my clients and family members for a written explanation of *Reframing***,** a subtle transformation began to undulate…like the gentle lapping of waves on a remote and tranquil beach. A location of safety where microcosmic grains of sand melded together to create an impenetrable barrier to isolation!

My own understanding of Reframing continues to serve me. Recognition of the power of choice truly took centre stage. *My Shadow still holds the space for me to reflect on the relationship that my sisters and I shared in that basement, so long ago.* Here were three little girls who lived life with faith—a faith that passes all understanding! By forming an independent alliance through their desire for each other and for home (a safe place *within*) they were successful in accumulating the tools necessary to ensure the manifestation of their perceived purpose and its execution, *even while lacking conscious recognition.*

Jan (Jeanette Marie), the eldest of us three girls, married young and was the mother of two children. In her forties she honoured a lifetime desire to become an Elementary School Teacher, bringing with her a wide variety of life experiences to draw upon. Jan also worked in the capacity of Early Literacy for two years where she was able to provide a different and refreshing take on children, and how best to serve their needs. Now retired, Jan continues her commitment to children as an author of children's books. Jan and her friend Deborah Kekewich, who was also a teacher and has a background in publishing, joined their passion for children to create and publish six wonderful books for the express purpose of offering joy, adventure and education. Their unique publishing style created a platform for future children's authors to incorporate, offering parents an effective way to engage interactively with their children.

Karon (Belinda), the youngest of us three girls, also married young and was the mother of two children. Karon's sense of service came in strong and compassionately. An early relationship with traditional religion, the teachings of Joseph Campbell, Buddhism, and a healthy desire to understand the bible lead Karon into the field of holistic healing. While teaching and educating as a Reiki Master, Karon began to recognize a correlation with the body, its energy centres (the Chakra system) and how one perceives the world around them. 'Mastery' is what Karon developed as a healer. One morning in prayer and meditation, Karon asked for guidance and an understanding of what she was here to do in this lifetime, she received the following message: *"You Karon*

SPEAK KINDLY TO YOUR SHADOW

are not here <u>To Do</u> anything. You are here to <u>be</u> an example of compassion in the world."

I must acknowledge these two wonderful ladies and sisters of mine in the completion of this book. Jan and Karon were instrumental in bringing this book to life, and I cannot thank them enough.

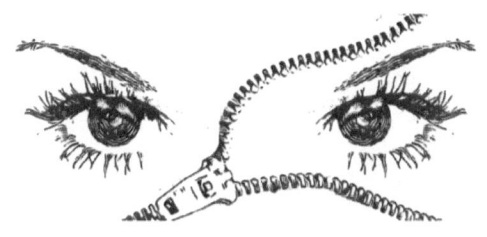

SANDRA ANNE DAVIS

RESOURCES

The Book of Runes by Ralph H Blum (St. Martin's Press, 1983).

Earth Dance Drum by Blackwolf and Gina Jones (Commune-A-Key Publishing, 1996).

How To Manifest by Gill Thackray (Ten Speed Press, 2022).

Love Is in the Earth: A Kaleidoscope of Crystals by Melody (Earth Love Pub house, 1995).

Medicine Cards by Jamie Sams & David Carson (St. Martin's Press, 1999).

The Sacred Path Cards by Jamie Sams (Harper One Publishing, 1990).

Practicing Peace In Times Of War by Pema Chödrön (Shambhala, 2006).

The Undiscovered Self by Carl Jung (Berkley, 2006).

You Can Have It All by Arnold Patent (Beyond Words Publishing, 1995).

SANDRA ANNE DAVIS

ENDNOTES

---

[i] My meaning of a Spiritual Counsellor: I have been sharing my understanding of the magnificence I witness of humanity and its unlimited potential for many years now. I began by counselling the students that came to me through Centennial College. My awareness of their light and the extent of their passion and desire became evident over the years. What I came to observe was a deep desire by the people around me to be recognized and seen. Not for someone else's perception of them, but a desire that ran below the surface of all their interactions. Spirituality was a term that seemed to express *"the quality of being concerned with the human spirit or soul as opposed to material or physical things."* They

were all in search of something that connects them to the natural environment.

I soon found that I had a role to play on the stage of life! In my capacity as a counsellor I was able to offer a mirror to those souls in need of reflection. In the words of I-Ching: "The perfect man is but a mirror. He leans neither forward nor backward. He remains unchanged."

Standing firmly in place in a power stance with the truth as I perceived it to be, created a healthy arrogance that allowed me to trust and believe in myself. All that was required of me was to hold a space for these individuals to see and recognize their magnificence. The perfection of their imperfections and its significance in the grand scheme of things!

I have come to believe that life's purpose is true Sovereignty! And accept that the only access to sovereignty is through alignment with God. It is my belief that all of us, as a humanity, require no other pursuit or purpose than to trust the God-Self reflected in our mirror…for this is the way home.

[ii] THE SACRED HOOP: One Circle. One word. One vision. One truth. Native tradition honours the Circle, for here lies the secret of life itself, the spirit of the Creator. The Hoop Dance is about the Circle. The Sacred Hoop is the circumference of the Medicine Wheel, a healing symbol of balance. For more information on the Medicine Wheel, see *Listen to the Drum: Blackwolf Shares his Medicine* and *The Healing Drum.*

We live above circles, beneath circles, within circles, through circles. Earth Mother, Grandfather Sun, Grandmother Moon, and the Stars are all circular. The seasons are cyclical. The water cycles. Life carries us around the Sacred Hoop. The Seven Directions point to the circular way of life. (*Earth Dance Drum* by Blackwolf and Gina Jones. Commune-A-Key Publishing, 1996. Pg 307 & 308)

[iii] "Vacuum" is a common translation of the Latin phrase *horror vacui*. "Nature abhors a vacuum", which is a concept in physics and philosophy attributed to Aristotle. It means that nature requires all space to be filled, and that empty spaces do not occur naturally, because denser material will fill them. The idea is that there's a natural law that says that nature won't let there be a void; empty space is always taken up by something. When something is removed, it's immediately replaced with something else…(Drew Amoroso Aug 11th podcast EP 018 2020).

[iv] In Jungian psychology, the ego, anima, and animus are key concepts related to the psyche. The ego is the conscious centre of personality, while the anima and Animus represent unconscious archetypes of the opposite gender within each individual. The anima is the feminine archetype in men and the

animus is the masculine archetype in women. *Wikipedia, The archetypes of the Anima & Animus, Centre of Applied Studies, Jungian 4 February, 2024.*

[v] **Numerology: Spiritual meaning of seven.** The number seven is connected to intuition, wisdom, growing self-awareness, spiritual revelations and big shifts that can have a powerful impact on your life. It's a number that serves as a bridge or connection between our mortal realm and higher places.

Psychology of seven: We all live our lives through 10 cycles, each lasting seven years from the time we are born until 70 and beyond. Throughout them, we pass through challenges, learn profound lessons, sharpen our physical & emotional instincts, and discover spiritual growth (www.wity.tech).

There is a universal understanding of the impact that society has invested in the number seven. It is well researched and written about. The basis of this specific number is expressed in many cultures and myths. For our purpose, my Native Teachings have prepared me and taught me of the importance of being the seventh generation in this lifetime! They constantly encourage us to remain cognizant of the responsibility to effect the changes, the healing and to impart our wisdom, to make ready the way for the next seven generations to come.

[vi] British euphemism that refers to a foolish or inept person.

[vii] Born in the family castle of Xavier, near Pamplona in Basque area of Spanish Navarre on April 7, he was sent to the University of Paris, secured his licentiate in 1528, and met Ignatius Loyola! Francis became one of the seven who in 1534, at Montmartre founded the society of Jesus ORDER OF THE JESUITS! In 1536 Francis joined Ignatius in Venice and was ordained in 1537, went to Rome in 1538. In

1540 the pope formally recognized the Society and ordered Francis and FR. Simon Rodriguez, to the Far East as the first Jesuit missionaries. King John III kept FR. Simon in Lisbon, but Francis, after a year's voyage, six months of which were spent at Mozambique where he preached and gave aid to the sick, eventually arrived in Goa, India in 1542 with FR. Paul of Camerino, an Italian, and Francis Mansihas, a Portuguese. There he began preaching to the natives and attempted to reform his fellow Europeans, living among the natives and adopting their customs on his travels. During the next decade he converted tens of thousands to Christianity. He visited the Paravas at the tip of India, near Cape Comorin, Tuticorin (1542), Malacca (1545), the Moluccas near New Guinea Morotai near the Philippines (1546-47), and Japan (1549-51). In 1551, India and the East were set up as a separate province and Ignatius made Francis its first provincial. In 1552 he set out for China, landed on the island of Sancian within sight of his goal, but died before he reached the mainland. Working against great difficulties, language problems (contrary to legend, he had no proficiency in in foreign tongues), inadequate funds and lack of cooperation, often facing resistance from European officials, he left the mark of his missionary zeal and energy on areas which clung to Christianity for centuries. He was canonised in 1622 and proclaimed patron of all foreign missions by Pope Pius X. F. D. Dec 3. (www.catholic.org)

[viii] Sweats vary from purification and cleansing to healing sweats. It is said that during the sweat lodge ceremony, the individual needs of each participant are "responded to". *Anishnawbe Health, Toronto.*

[ix] The Red Road means a deep commitment to living life in the best way possible with an

intrinsic respect for others, oneself and the Creator. (www.theredroad.org)

[x] There are many symbols in this dream/vision sequence that hold meaning for me. For example, I understand the meaning of the colour white in a dream can mean the language of our soul and how we change and provoke thoughts. White also represents purity. White shoes are powerful objects of identity and desire. They are also a fascinating indicator of a spiritual journey. Therefore, the white dress and shoes provided insight as to how I was feeling in waking life and with my own self-identity. I think it is also worth noting that shoes are connected to the ground…my reminder to stay grounded.

In some dream dictionaries, shoes themselves are presented as hidden aspects of our internal system, reminding *me* to move forward in life; and the baby shoes were indicating a need to refocus my intention on a spiritual path that was for my highest good and the highest good of all!

The presence of socks can symbolize comfort and warmth, and a desire for comfort and security in your life and the symbolization of the parts of yourself that you keep hidden or covered up! It is my belief that the act of dreaming about socks is indicating a need to explore these aspects of my own life.

Spiritually, a baby boy in a dream represents masculine energy and strength, meaning the need for being more action-oriented, focused and developing a strong willpower.

Lauri Quinn Loewenburg says, "Usually baby dreams represent growth and development, either with you personally or with something that you're working on. It's a message from your subconscious saying this new thing is great, it's time to focus and nurture it. It's time to get busy."

[xi] Red meaning: Red symbolizes energy, action, confidence, courage and change. Red brings passion and strength to your relationships, your life and your work.

Red represents the root chakra. Our foundation Chakra. It develops in the first seven years of life and deals with survival and security needs. When the root is out of balance, we may feel insecure, unsafe and even disconnected from reality *(Sarah Regan, www.mindbodygreen.com)*.

[xii] **Right side** energy blockages may indicate a father wound or over-giving, putting others first, and sacrificing personal needs. It may also reveal a resistance to being true to yourself and sharing your light with the world. This can lead to exhaustion, frustration and anger. **The left side** represents the feminine principle in both Men and Women. It indicates the ability to ask for help, to receive or to

surrender; to nourish and care for others; to be tender and caring; to be creative and artistic; to listen to and trust your own wisdom. (www.bookshelf.ca)

[xiii] Water represents vulnerability

[xiv] Sun represents authenticity

[xv] Deer meaning in the Medicine Cards book by Jamie Sams: *Gentleness has amazing strength. Where some would dominate, others are sweet and compassionate and this gives us hope. A gentle person is cool, clear water on a hot day—a refreshing change from hostile attitudes. How many times we have met someone we wanted to admire but couldn't. They would not trust us to see beyond their protective walls. Caring and friendship was sorely needed but bitterly ignored. To understand these things makes us gentle. It gives us the touch we need with every age.*

Young and old yearn to hear a voice that tells them they are so important, so loved, that nothing could make us turn from them. A gentle word is warm sunshine to every heart, a touch that is never forgotten.

[xvi] Ode'imin the heart berry is an Ojibway word that refers to the strawberry. The strawberry is used to teach us about the heart and love. They were given the name ode'imin because of the heart shape; ode means heart and min refers to berry. (www.itcme.org)

[xvii] Amber Stone meaning continued:

"...It is a sacred stone to both Native American and Eastern Indians. It has been used in the fire ceremonies of ancient tribal healers. It was burned, beginning in the mediaeval days, as a fumigant and as an incense to clear the environment of negativity. It aligns the ethereal energies to the physical, mental, and emotional bodies, providing for an even flow of perfect order to the requirements of the Earth plane while balancing the electromagnetics of the physical body. It has been used in the treatment of goiter and other dis-eases of the throat. It has also been successful in the treatment of disorders of the kidneys and bladder. In ancient times it was used as a penicillin-type remedy, ground and ingested or soaked [as in an elixir] and subsequently drunk. Vibrates to the number 3." (*Love is in the Earth* by Melody).

[xviii] Many people feel uneasy about using Tarot cards. That's due to misunderstanding and myth. Tarot reading is an ancient mystical practice used across many cultures, dating all the way back to the fifteenth century. Think of the cards as a tool to focus your thinking, enabling you to tap into divine wisdom as you explore a particular goal or issue that you want to manifest. (Gill Thackray, *How To Manifest*, 2022).

[xix] This is a dream/vision that took place in my living room in Vancouver in 2003. I was lying on my couch just dozing when I opened my eyes and saw my inner child, the orphan within! She had previously presented herself to me years before (1991) in a dream while living and working in Florida.

At that time the dream was rather unsettling, because in the dream I was responsible for her welfare, but I was too busy writing (which I was actually doing a lot of during that time!) and became distracted. Suddenly there was a knock at the door of my hotel room. When I opened the door, I found the hotel manager holding my little girl's hand. The man was well dressed and very handsome. In contrast to him, my little girl had on a homemade smock dress with embroidery across the front of it. Her hair was unkempt and she looked thoroughly disheveled! She had a dirty face and, in her hand, she held a pudding cup with a spoon in it. She had pudding on her face around her little mouth. But there she stood looking at me with the happiest and brightest smile I've ever seen! The hotel manager went on to apologize for disturbing my writing, but when he found her wandering the halls unattended, he immediately felt a responsibility to provide her with something to eat and then to bring her home. I expressed my sincere gratitude to him for finding and feeding her. It was bizarre the way in which the three of us just stood there in the doorway looking at one another. My little girl still smiling brightly while this man and I smiled warmly and without edifice at one another.

SANDRA ANNE DAVIS

www.ingramcontent.com/pod-product-compliance
Lightning Source LLC
Chambersburg PA
CBHW060355080526
44583CB00012B/329